Joachim Klang

LEGO® BUILD YOUR OWN VEHICLES

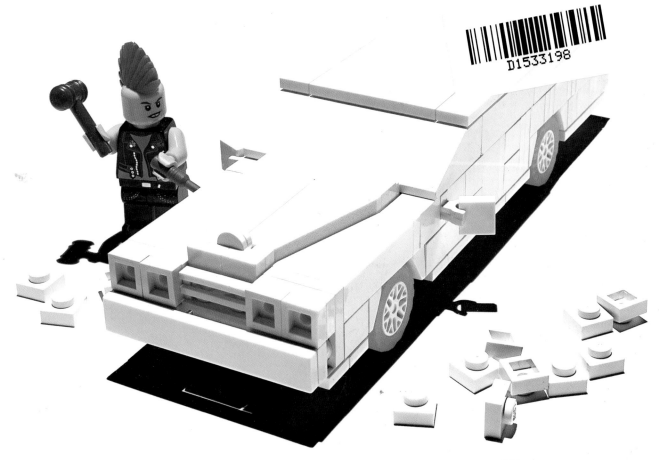

HEEL

Thanks to some pioneers and revolutionaries, some of whom we know in person and admire:

2LegoOrNot2Lego	Henrik Hoexbroe	marshal banana	Sirens-Of-Titan
Arvo Brothers	Homa	McBricker	Spencer_R
Bricksonwheels	Joe Meno	mijasper	T.Oechsner
bricktrix	Jojo	Misterzumbi	Théolego
Bruceywan	Karwik	Nannan Z	tnickolaus
Cole Blaq	lego_nabii	NENN	x_Speed
DecoJim	Legohaulic	„Orion Pax"	
Eastpole77	LEGOLAS	Pepa Quin	
Fredoichi	Legotrucks	RoccoB	
gambort	_lichtblau_	Sir Nadroj	

My special thanks for their support go to Lutz „El-Lutzo" Uhlmann for preparing the construction instructions, and to Christian Treczoks for building these amazing trees and shrubs which tremendously enrich the photographs.

HEEL Verlag GmbH
Gut Pottscheidt
53639 Königswinter
Germany
Tel.: +49 (0) 2223 9230-0
Fax: +49 (0) 2223 9230-13
E-Mail: info@heel-verlag.de
www.heel-verlag.de

© 2013 HEEL Verlag GmbH

Author: Joachim Klang
Layout and Design: Odenthal Illustration, www.odenthal-illustration.de
Cover Design: HEEL Verlag GmbH, Axel Mertens, Königswinter
Photographs: Thomas Schultze, www.thomas-schultze.de
Translation: Kim Maya and William Banks Sutton
Editor: Ulrike Reihn-Hamburger

Printed in Italy

ISBN 978-3-86852-766-7

Contents

This is **Joe**. He will be joining you throughout the book and helping you with tips and suggestions, when it gets more complicated. In the city, Joe has many friends, who all sooner or later come to his garage with their cars. This is a wonderful opportunity to show you, with detailed building instructions, how to use your LEGO® collection to produce detailed automobiles, race cars, pickups or tractors.

Foreword

First of all, thank you for the great popularity of our first volume, „The Big unofficial LEGO® Builder's Book – Build your own City", which we really enjoyed. An unbelievable number of LEGO® fans have contacted us in so many ways, inspiring us to continue. The professional models in miniature scale triggered considerable feedback, as was expected.

Therefore, in this second volume, I am especially dedicating myself to the topic of miniature vehicles to scale, and thus, I will show you my ideas for a sports car, a sedan, a tractor, a pick-up and—by popular demand—a classic car. Most of these model cars are so-called „fan models", which put considerably high value on originality and detail. This could mean that the models are not that stable. On the other hand, all of the models—other than the classic car, which is designed as a cabinet or standing model—move, meaning the wheels turn. I find this to be a good compromise for this book.

I have heard from many fans that they followed the building instructions to the letter. This makes me very happy and gives me the comfort that the building instructions are not that complicated and actually work. However, since the models are supposed to be ideas and inspirations for your own creations, I am presenting more variations on form and color in this book. Sometimes you might not have at hand the specific pieces in the color described. Thus, the photos provide varying ideas for your own imaginative solutions. I am happy if I can give your creativity and inventiveness food for thought.

Please feel free to give me constructive criticism and many new ideas.

Have fun building!

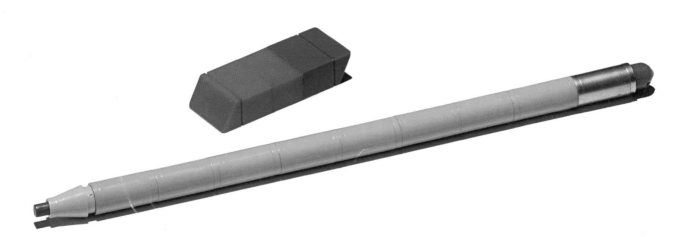

Sports car

Who hasn't dreamed of sports and racing cars as a child? Silver-plated exhaust pipes, a shiny front grille and slick tires ... Speaking of which, experts will immediately notice that very old tires from the 1960s were mounted on this classic racing car. However, the 2x2 rim allows for many other solutions.

Here is another example of how it pays to lift old stickers and scrap pieces. The number 22 was originally designed for a football jersey, but it works here really well.

Naturally, it is also possible to build this sports car in another color. Red is very common, chrome silver is not always available. I have decided on the typical Ferrari-red, or LEGO®-red, but you can try it out for yourself.

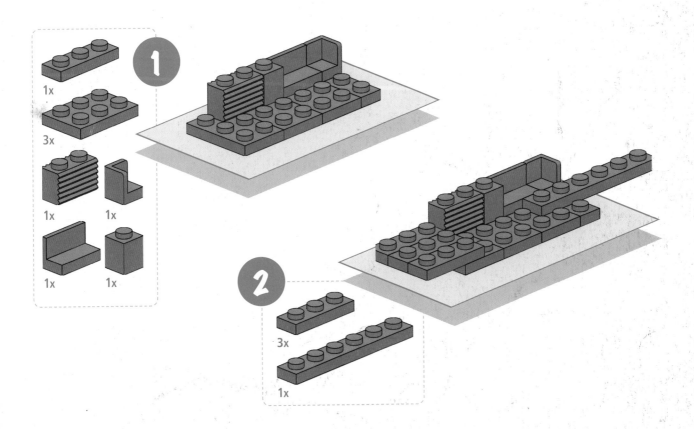

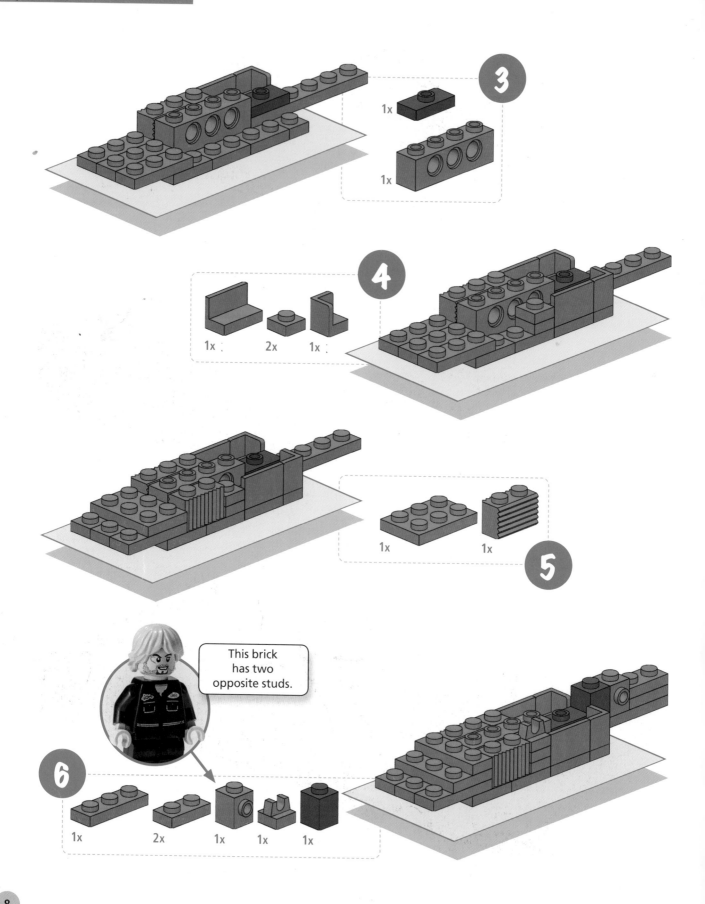

3

1x

1x

4

1x   2x   1x

5

1x   1x

This brick
has two
opposite studs.

6

1x   2x   1x   1x   1x

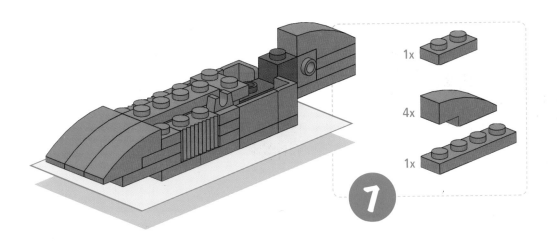

1x

4x

1x

7

8

1x

2x

1x

3x

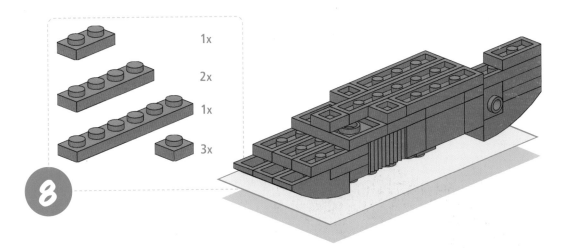

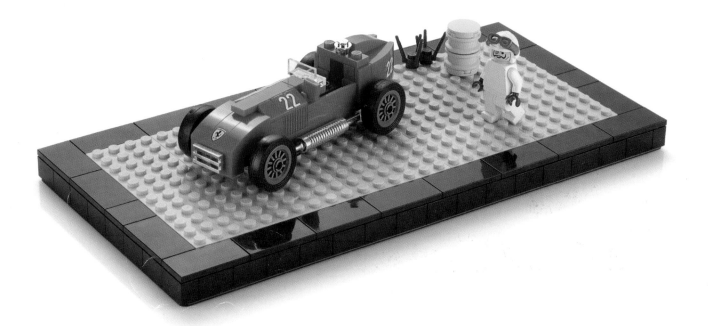

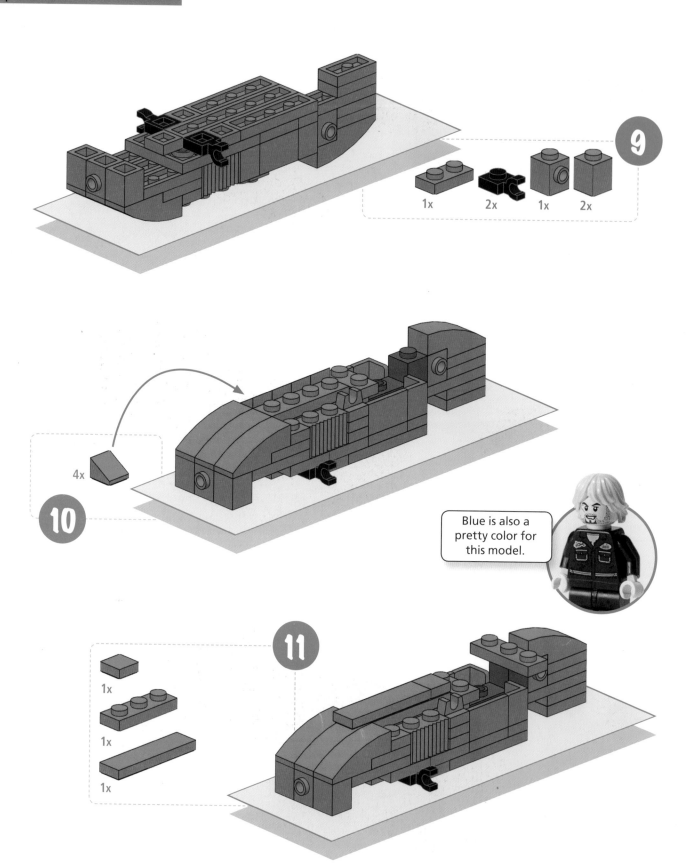

9

1x   2x   1x   2x

10

4x

Blue is also a
pretty color for
this model.

11

1x

1x

1x

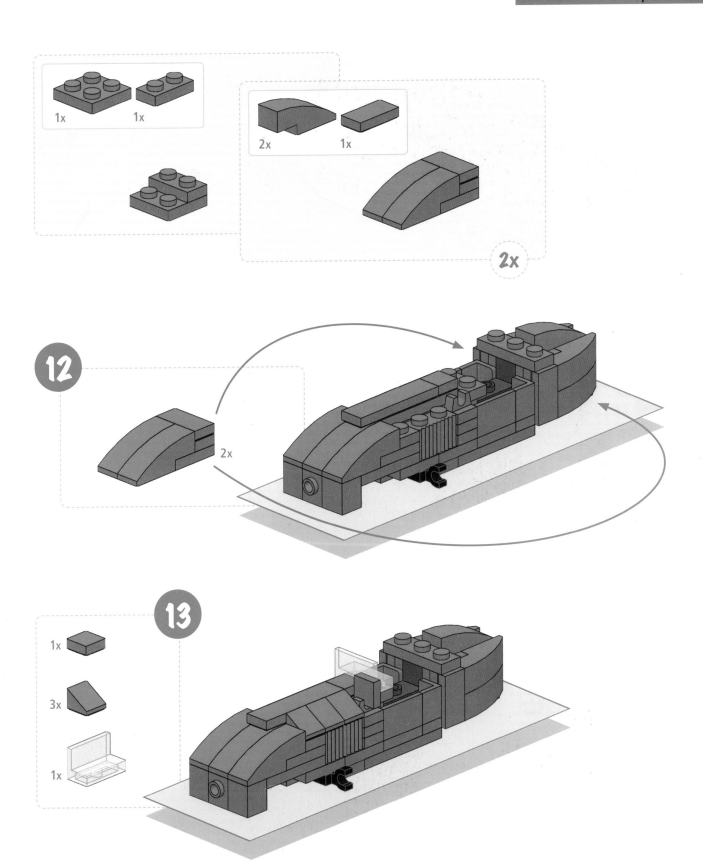

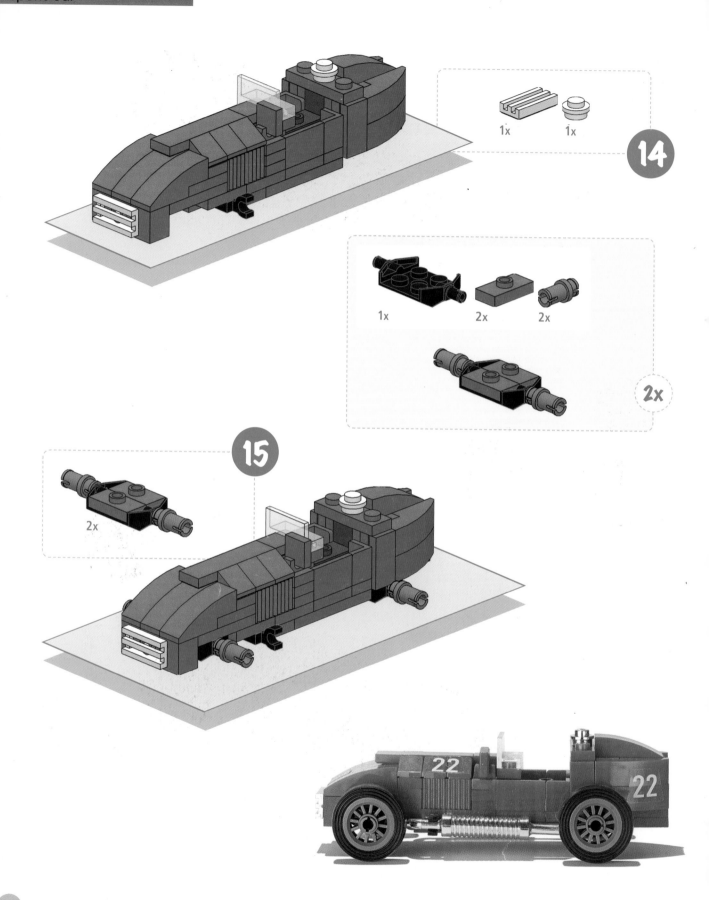

14

1x   1x

1x   2x   2x

2x

15

2x

22   22

16

2x

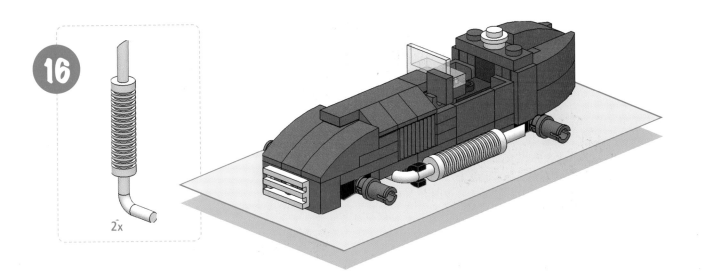

4x

1x

1x

17

4x

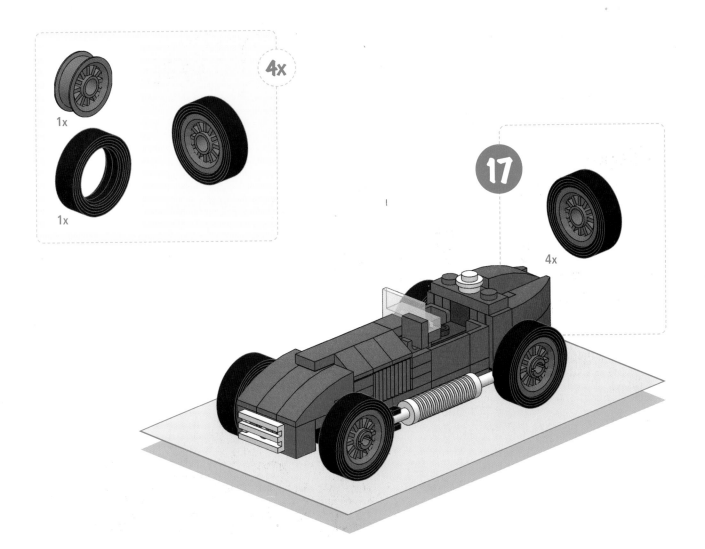

Parts List

1x

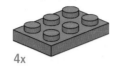
4x

1x

7x

1x

2x

3x

2x

1x

7x

4x

2x

2x

5x

1x

2x

2x

2x

1x

3x

2x

1x

2x

1x

4x

1x

1x

6x

4x

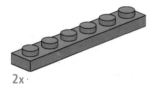
2x

8x

4x

Quantity	Color		Element	Element Name
1		Chrome Silver	2412b	Tile 1 x 2 Grille with Groove
1		Red	2431	Tile 1 x 4 with Groove
1		Red	2555	Tile 1 x 1 with Clip
2		Red	2877	Brick 1 x 2 with Grille
2		Red	30010	Panel 1 x 2 x 1 with Square Corners
3		Red	3005	Brick 1 x 1
1		Reddish Brown	3005	Brick 1 x 1
4		Dark-Gray	30155	Wheel Centre Spoked Small
4		Red	3021	Plate 2 x 3
2		Red	3022	Plate 2 x 2
7		Red	3023	Plate 1 x 2
5		Red	3024	Plate 1 x 1
2		Red	3069b	Tile 1 x 2 with Groove
2		Red	3070b	Tile 1 x 1 with Groove
4		Dark-Gray	32002	Technic Pin 3/4
6		Red	3623	Plate 1 x 3
2		Red	3666	Plate 1 x 6
1		Red	3701	Technic Brick 1 x 4 with Holes
3		Red	3710	Plate 1 x 4
4		Red	3794a	Plate 1 x 2 without Groove with 1 Centre Stud
1		Reddish Brown	3794a	Plate 1 x 2 without Groove with 1 Centre Stud
1		Chrome Silver	4073	Plate 1 x 1 Round
1		Red	47905	Brick 1 x 1 with Studs on Two Opposite Sides
1		Trans-Clear	4865a	Panel 1 x 2 x 1 with Square Corners
8		Red	50950	Slope Brick Curved 3 x 1
7		Red	54200	Slope Brick 31 1 x 1 x 2/3
2		Black	6019	Plate 1 x 1 with Clip Horizontal
2		Black	6157	Plate 2 x 2 with Wheels Holder Wide
2		Red	6231	Panel 1 x 1 x 1 Corner with Rounded Corners
2		Chrome Silver	71137	Exhaust Pipe
1		Red	87087	Brick 1 x 1 with Stud on 1 Side
4		Black		Tire 132 old

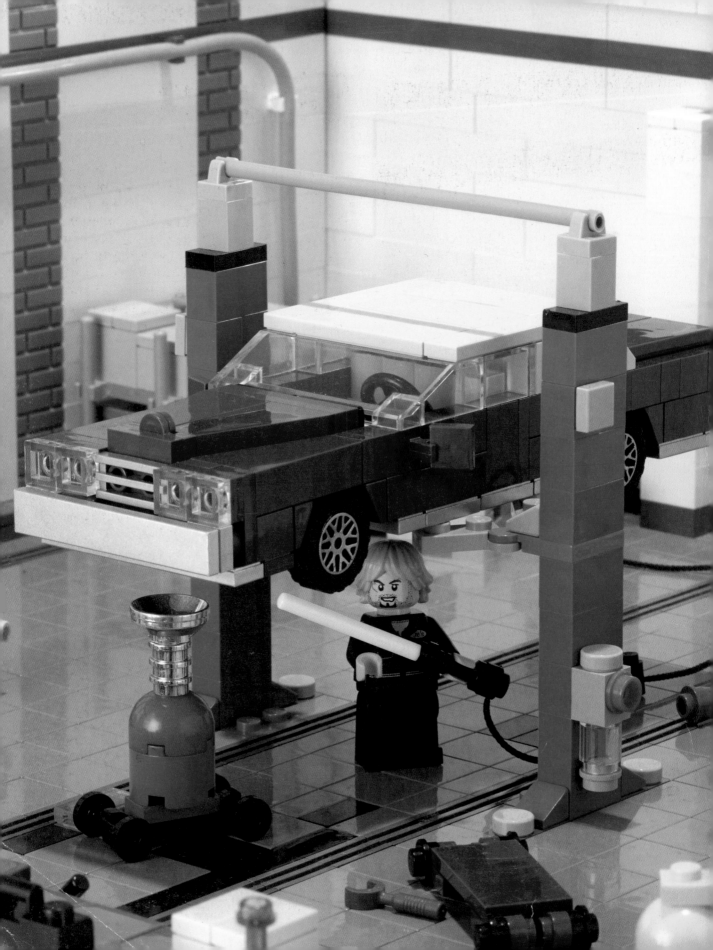

Sedan

The idea for the hood of this sedan has been buzzing around in my head for several years. I published an earlier version of this car on Brickshelf.com, but I was never satisfied with this original implementation. In the meantime, I have modified the car so much that it barely resembles my original model, if not only because many new pieces have been produced. However, the hood still goes back to my original idea. Sometimes, it takes only one idea to create a model in the end.

As you can see on the following pages, many color variations and modifications are possible for this model. For example, the roof is built so that it is easy to replace. Also, the rocker or the bumper can be easily replaced with other colored bricks. It is conceivable to use light gray, dark gray, silver or any other colored bricks in the respective body color — just use the possibilities that you have in your collection.

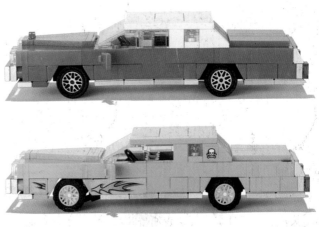

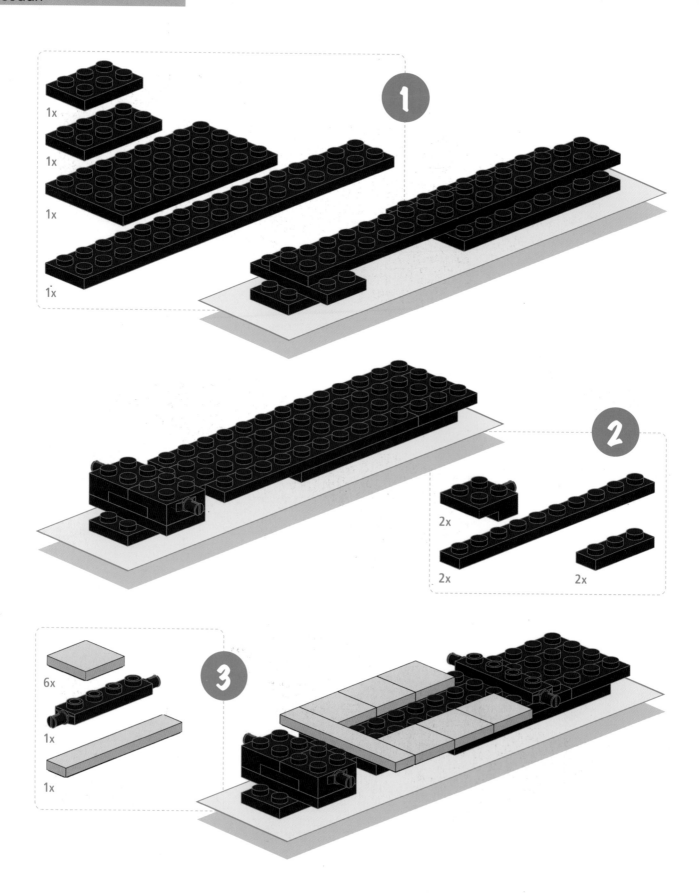

1x

1x

1x

1x

1

2

2x

2x

2x

6x

1x

1x

3

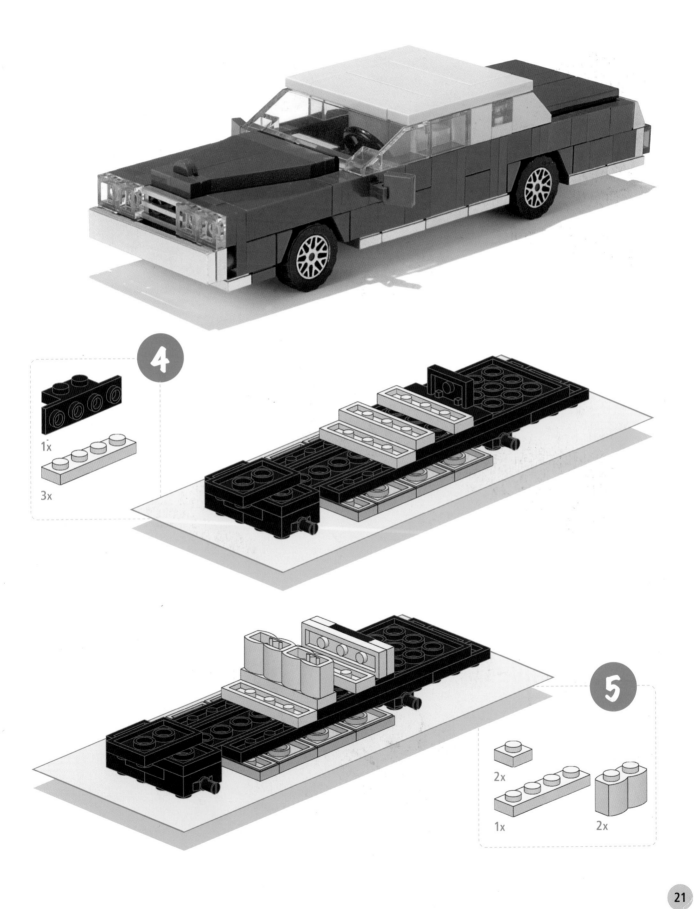

4

1x
3x

5

2x
1x
2x

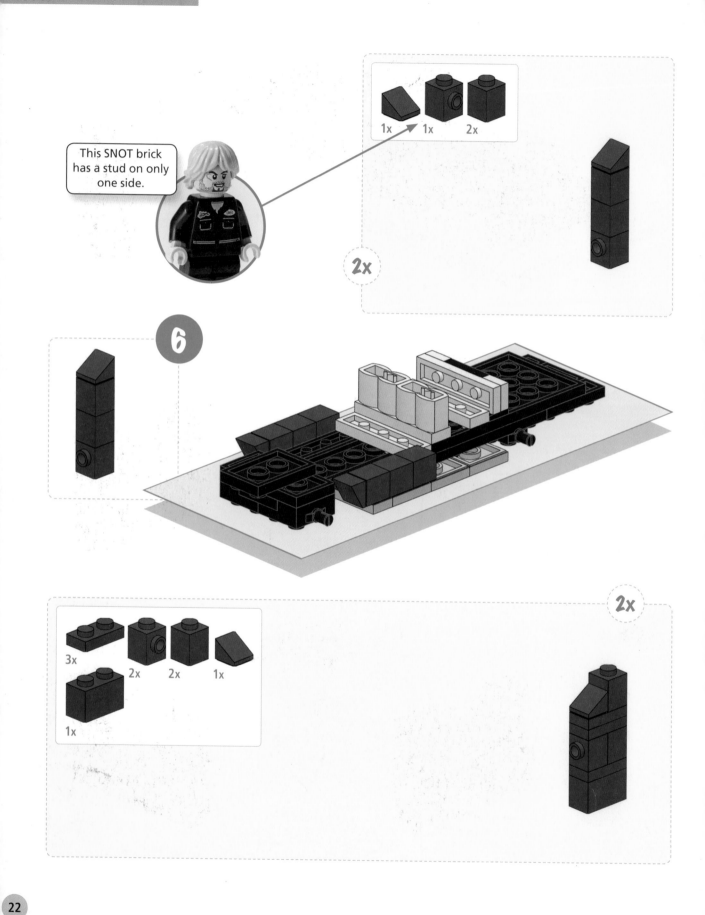

This SNOT brick has a stud on only one side.

1x 1x 2x

2x

6

3x 2x 2x 1x

1x

2x

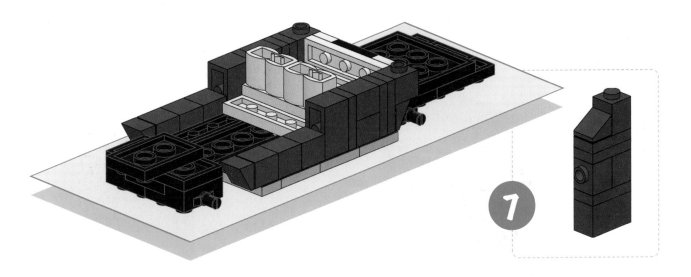

7

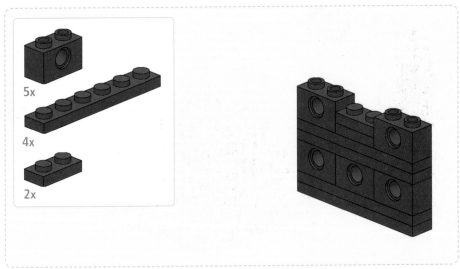

5x
4x
2x

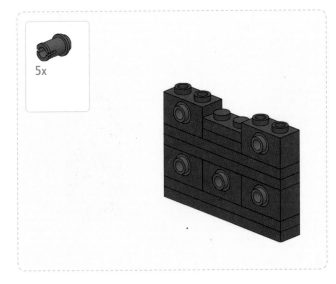

5x

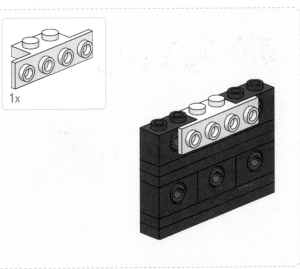

1x

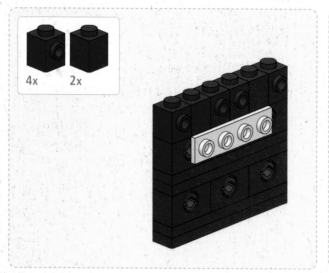

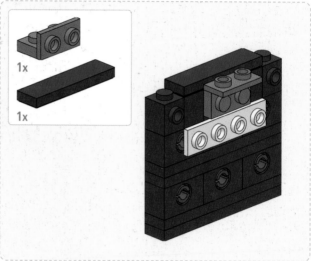

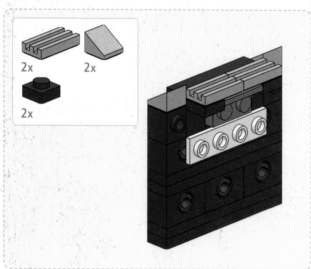

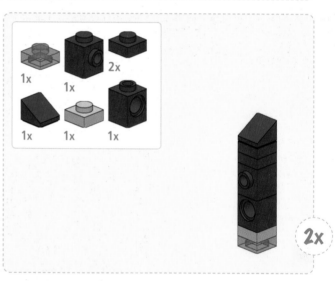

2x

This SNOT brick also has a stud on only one side.

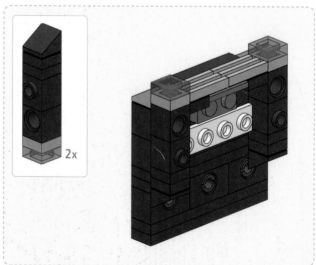

2x

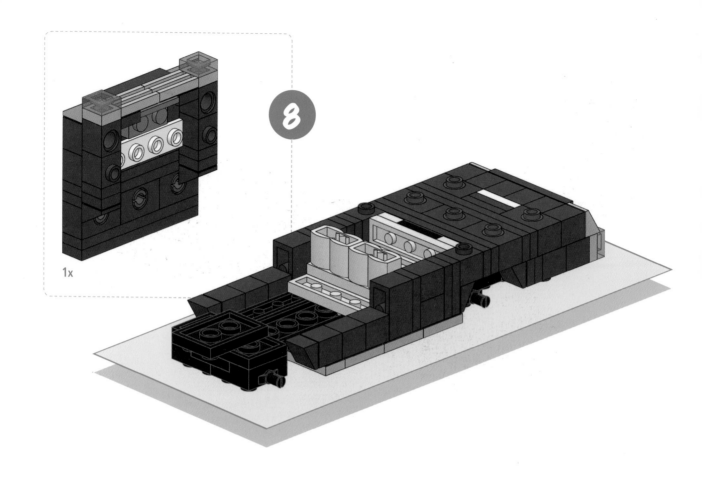

1x

8

If you don't have a
hinge plate at hand,
you can also use, for
example, a 2x2 plate.

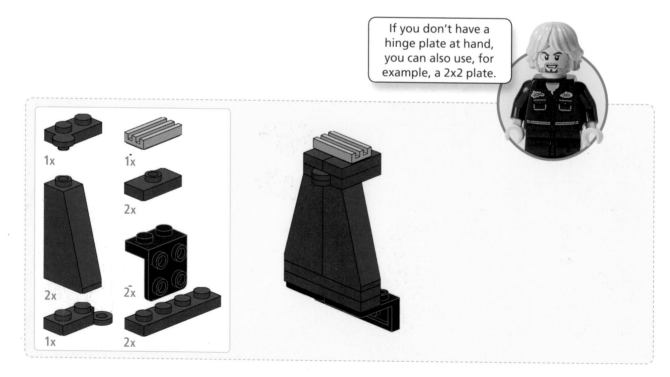

1x
1x
2x
2x
2x
1x
2x

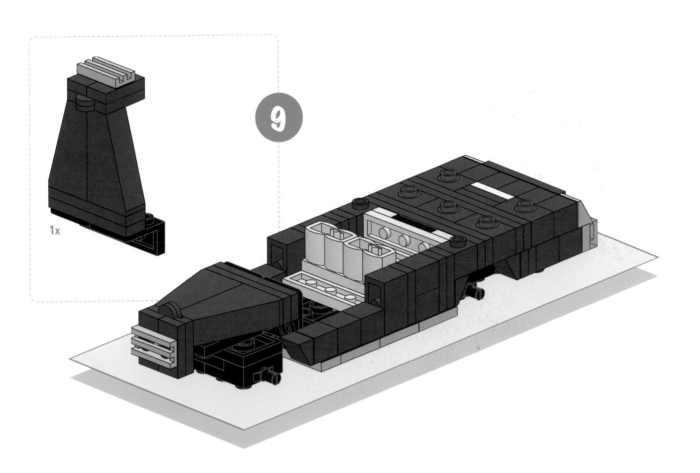

9

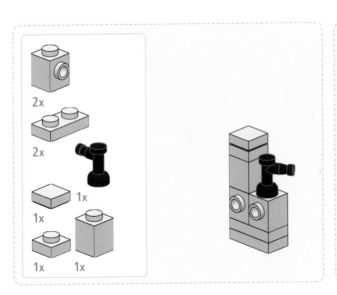

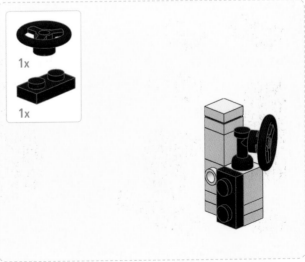

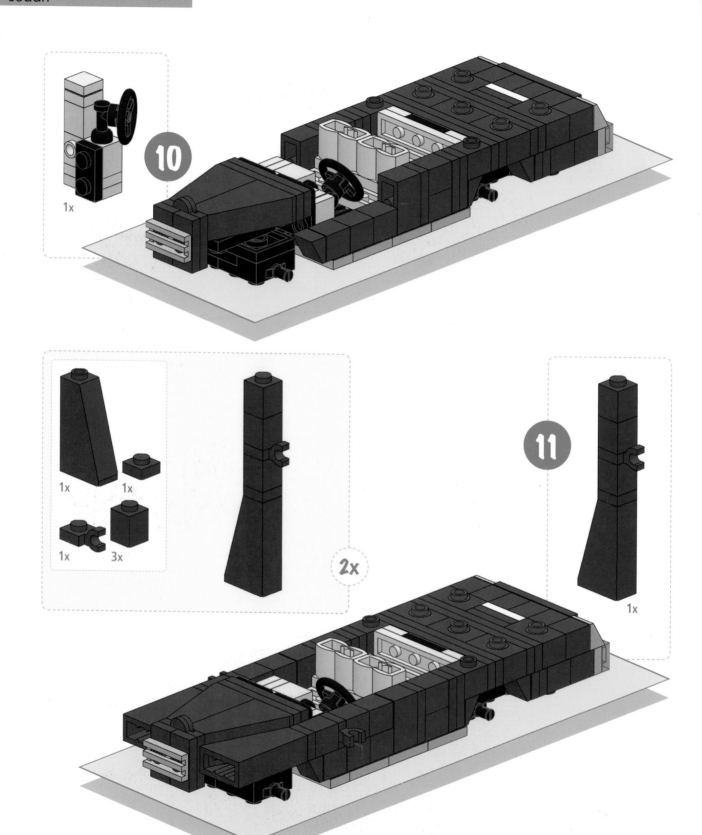

10

1x

1x   1x

1x   3x

2x

11

1x

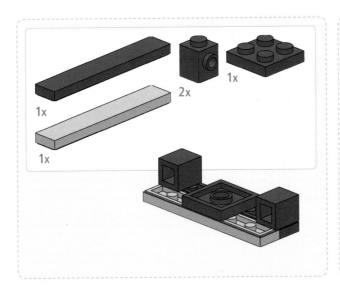

1x
1x
2x
1x

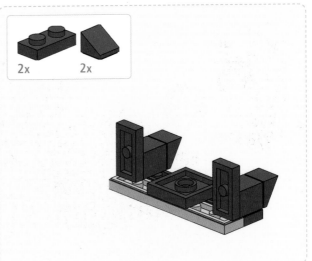

2x
2x

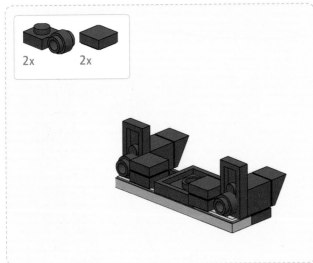

2x
2x

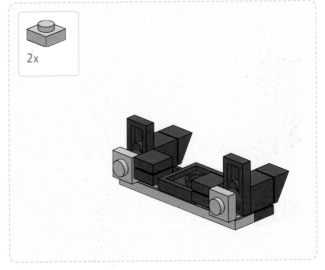

2x

2x

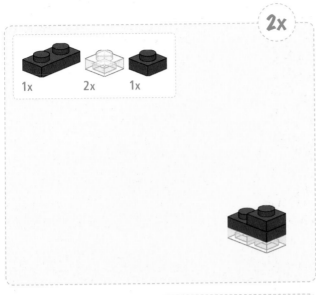

1x   2x   1x

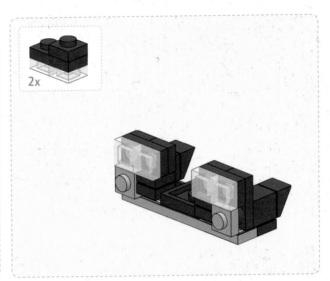

2x

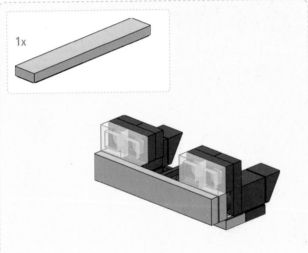

1x

The model can be varied with some stickers.

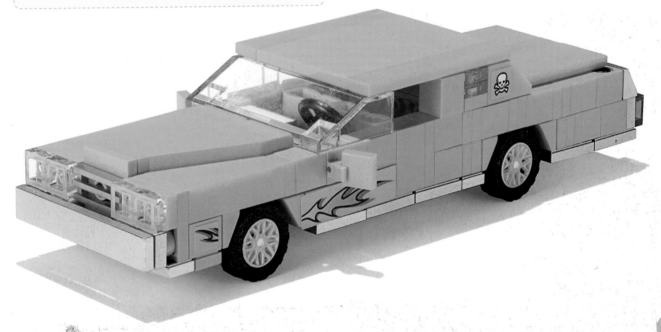

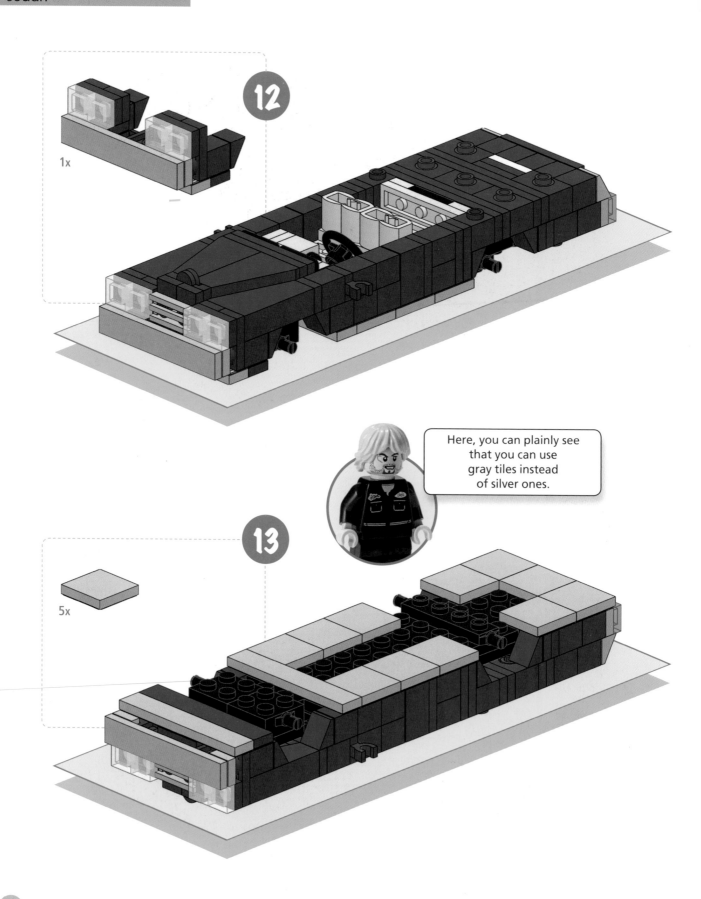

12

1x

13

5x

Here, you can plainly see that you can use gray tiles instead of silver ones.

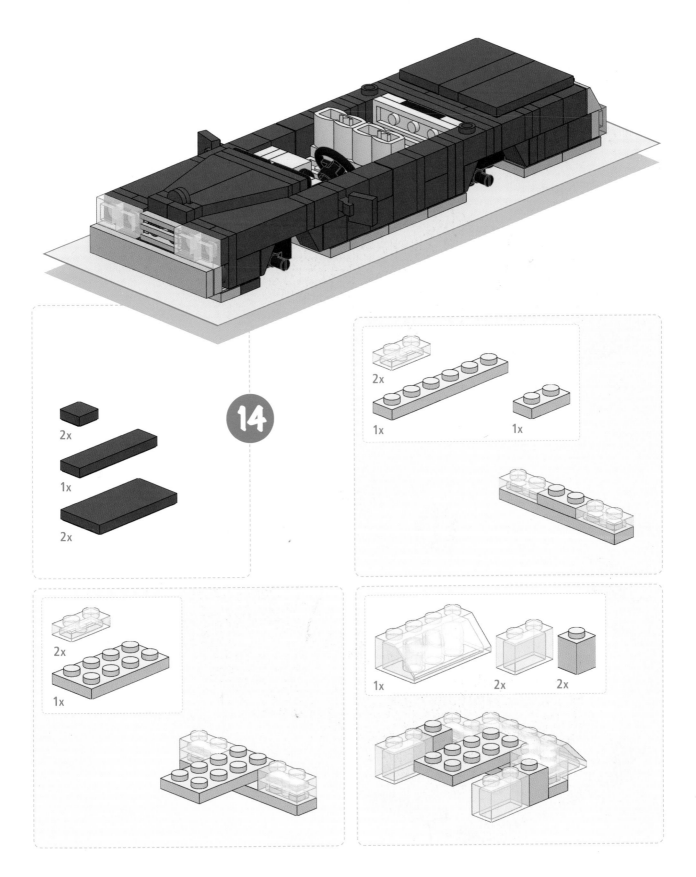

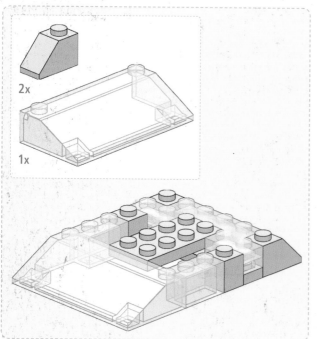

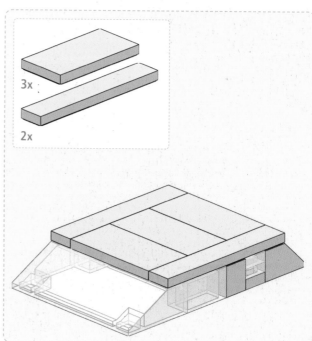

2x
1x

3x
2x

1x

15

The roof is only held on with two studs, so that you can easily replace it later with a different colored one.

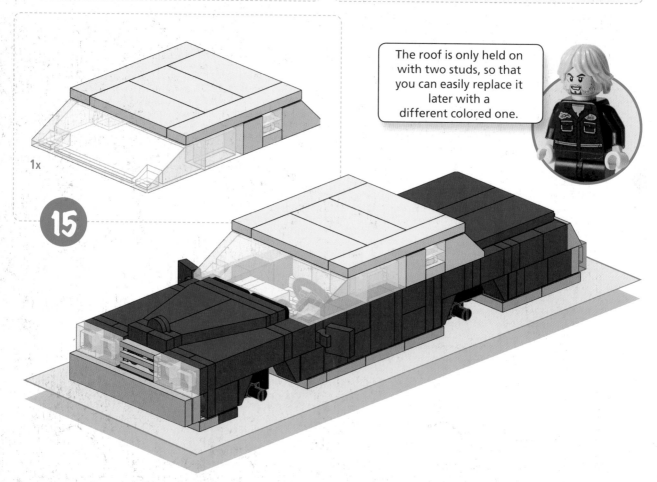

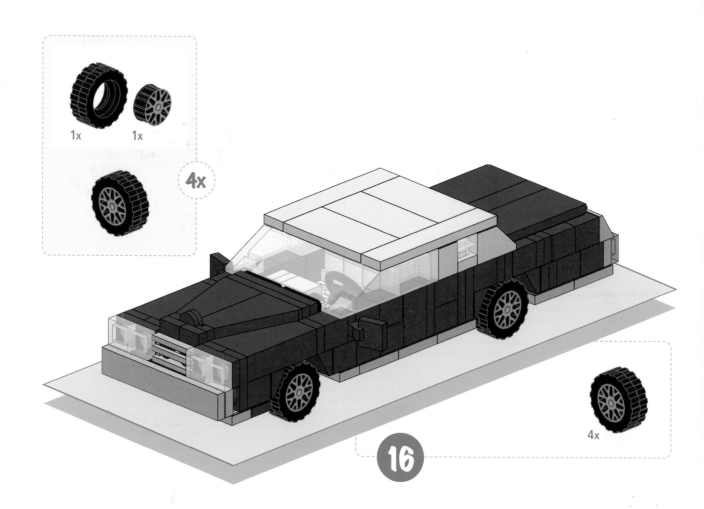

1x 1x

4x

16

4x

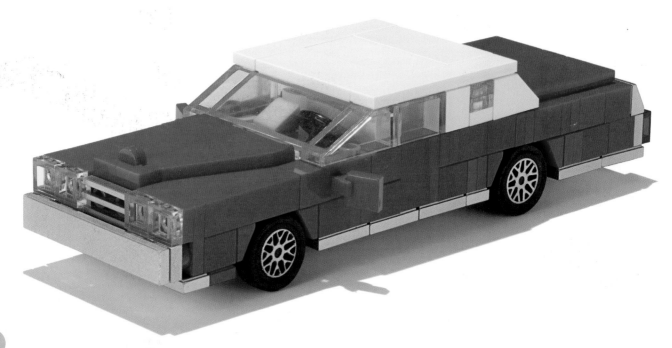

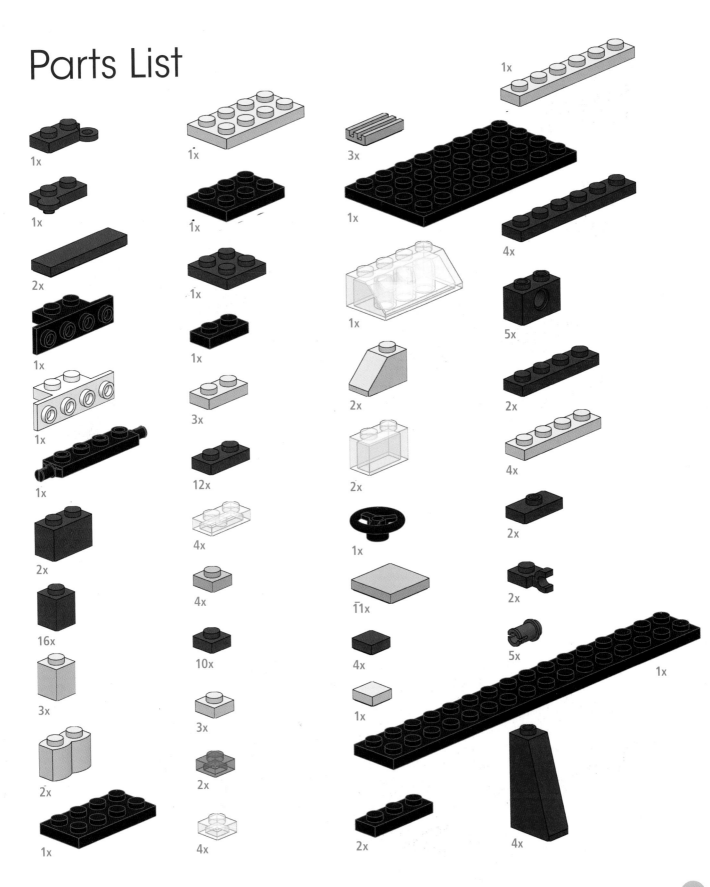

Parts List

1x

1x

1x

2x

1x

3x

5x

1x

2x

1x

1x

2x

1x

1x

1x

2x

4x

3x

2x

1x

2x

12x

2x

4x

2x

4x

4x

2x

16x

10x

11x

5x

4x

3x

3x

1x

2x

1x

2x

1x

4x

2x

4x

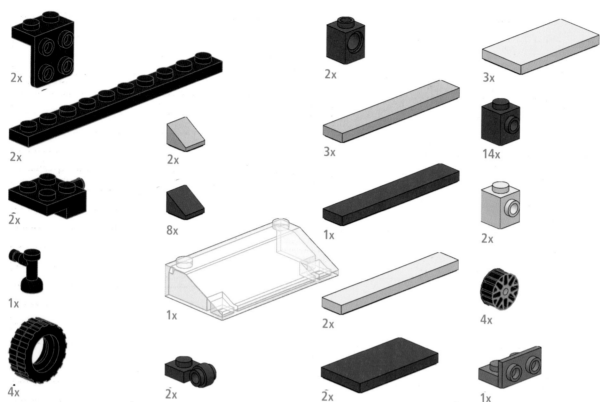

Quantity		Color	Element	Element Name
1		Reddish Brown	2429	Hinge Plate 1 x 4 Base
1		Reddish Brown	2430	Hinge Plate 1 x 4 Top
2		Reddish Brown	2431	Tile 1 x 4 with Groove
1		Black	2436a	Bracket 1 x 2 - 1 x 4 Type 1
1		White	2436a	Bracket 1 x 2 - 1 x 4 Type 1
1		Black	2926	Plate 1 x 4 with Wheels Holder
2		Reddish Brown	3004	Brick 1 x 2
16		Reddish Brown	3005	Brick 1 x 1
3		Tan	3005	Brick 1 x 1
2		Tan	30136	Brick 1 x 2 Log
1		Black	3020	Plate 2 x 4
3		Tan	3020	Plate 2 x 4
1		Black	3021	Plate 2 x 3
1		Reddish Brown	3022	Plate 2 x 2
1		Black	3023	Plate 1 x 2
3		Tan	3023	Plate 1 x 2
12		Reddish Brown	3023	Plate 1 x 2
4		Trans-Clear	3023	Plate 1 x 2
4		Metallic Silver	3024	Plate 1 x 1
10		Reddish Brown	3024	Plate 1 x 1

3	Tan	3024	Plate 1 x 1
2	Trans-Red	3024	Plate 1 x 1
4	Trans-Clear	3024	Plate 1 x 1
3	Metallic Silver	30244	Tile 1 x 2 Grille with Groove
1	Black	3035	Plate 4 x 8
1	Trans-Clear	3037	Slope Brick 45 2 x 4
2	Tan	3040b	Slope Brick 45 2 x 1
2	Trans-Clear	3065	Brick 1 x 2 without Centre Stud
1	Black	30663	Car Steering Wheel Large
11	Metallic Silver	3068b	Tile 2 x 2 with Groove
4	Reddish Brown	3070b	Tile 1 x 1 with Groove
1	Tan	3070b	Tile 1 x 1 with Groove
2	Black	3623	Plate 1 x 3
1	Tan	3666	Plate 1 x 6
4	Reddish Brown	3666	Plate 1 x 6
5	Reddish Brown	3700	Technic Brick 1 x 2 with Hole
2	Reddish Brown	3710	Plate 1 x 4
4	Tan	3710	Plate 1 x 4
2	Reddish Brown	3794a	Plate 1 x 2 without Groove with 1 Centre Stud
2	Reddish Brown	4081b	Plate 1 x 1 with Clip Light Type 2
5	Blue	4274	Technic Pin 1/2
1	Black	4282	Plate 2 x 16
4	Reddish Brown	4460	Slope Brick 75 2 x 1 x 3
2	Black	44728	Bracket 1 x 2 - 2 x 2
2	Black	4477	Plate 1 x 10
2	Black	4488	Plate 2 x 2 with Wheel Holder
1	Black	4599	Tap 1 x 1
4	Black	51011	Tyre 6.4/ 75 x 8 Shallow Offset Tread
2	Metallic Silver	54200	Slope Brick 31 1 x 1 x 2/3
8	Reddish Brown	54200	Slope Brick 31 1 x 1 x 2/3
1	Trans-Clear	58181	Slope Brick 33 3 x 6 without Inner Walls
2	Reddish Brown	6019	Plate 1 x 1 with Clip Horizontal
2	Reddish Brown	6541	Technic Brick 1 x 1 with Hole
3	Metallic Silver	6636	Tile 1 x 6
1	Reddish Brown	6636	Tile 1 x 6
2	Tan	6636	Tile 1 x 6
2	Reddish Brown	87079	Tile 2 x 4 with Groove
3	Tan	87079	Tile 2 x 4 with Groove
14	Reddish Brown	87087	Brick 1 x 1 with Stud on 1 Side
2	Tan	87087	Brick 1 x 1 with Stud on 1 Side
4	Black	93595c01	Wheel Rim 6.4 x 11 with 8 Silver Y-Shaped Spokes
1	Dark Bluish Gray	99780	Bracket 1 x 2 - 1 x 2 Down

Telephone booth

The construction of this telephone booth was so much fun when constructing the photo backgrounds that a guide to make it should not be missed. Naturally, you can use other colors here as well; gray works instead of silver, for example.

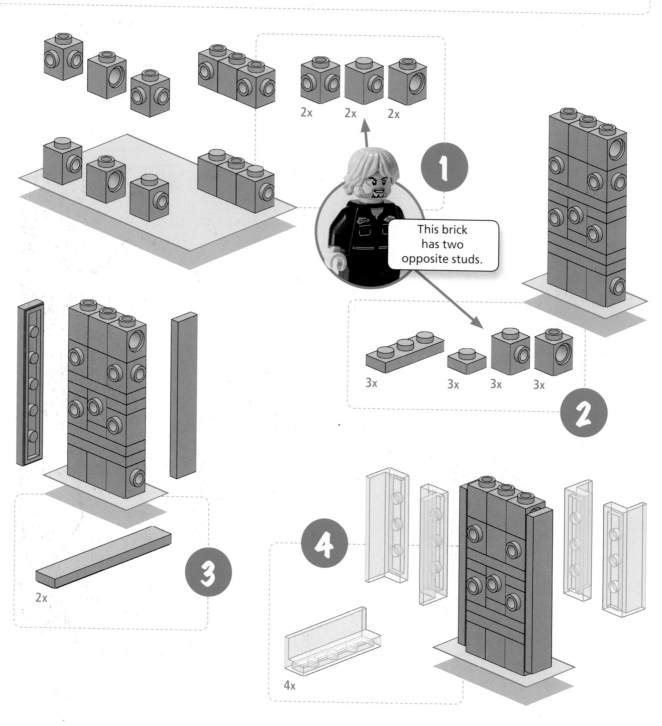

This brick has two opposite studs.

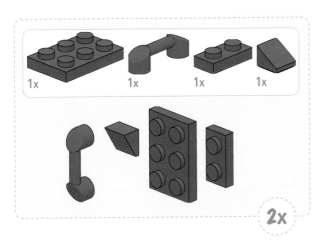

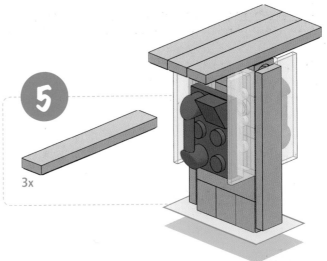

Tractor

Naturally, there have to be building instructions for a tractor in such a book! Almost every kid has one of these work vehicles in a small or large model to play with or ride. That's why this idea made sense. After all, I grew up in the country and was always fascinated with these powerful machines.

Here, the color variations are endless. Different wheels, roofs and body colors alone provide numerous variants. Even original tractors often were combined with roofs in different colors and from different manufacturers. The photos will show you several possibilities and encourage your own color combinations.

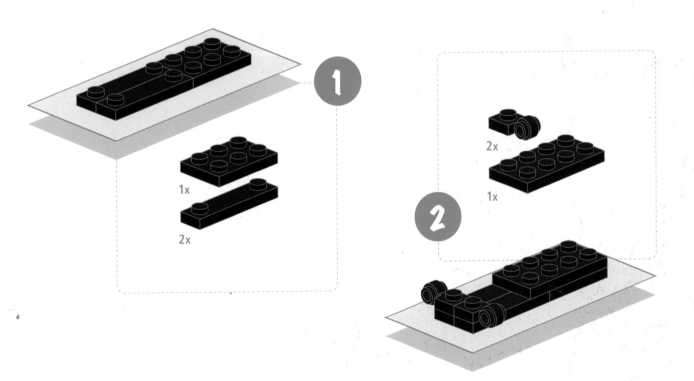

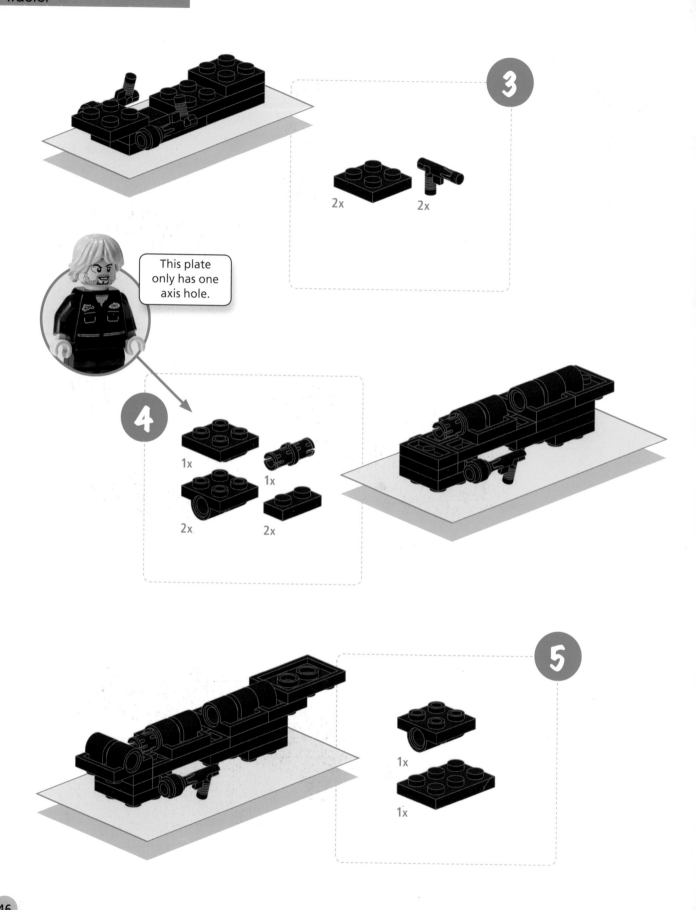

3

This plate only has one axis hole.

2x   2x

4

1x   1x

2x   2x

5

1x

1x

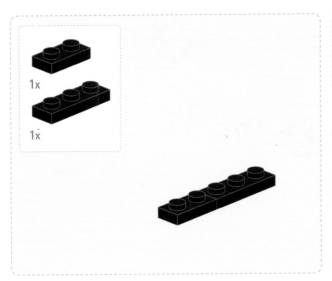

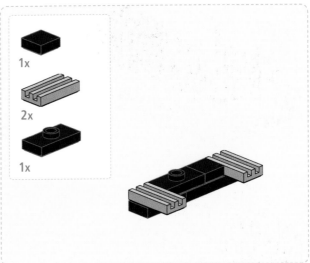

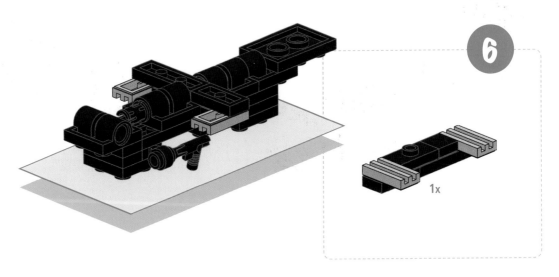

6

1x

7

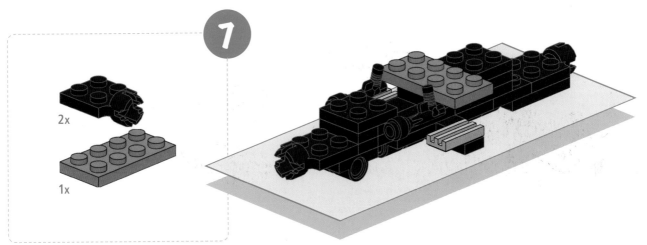

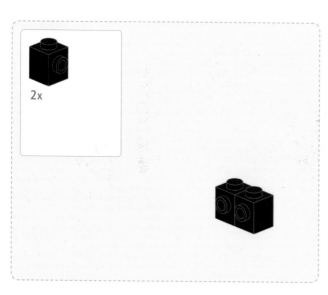

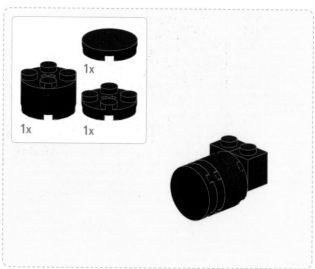

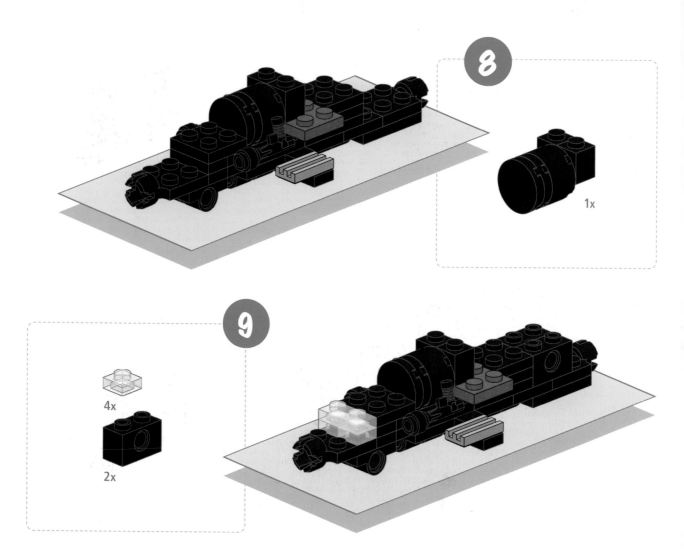

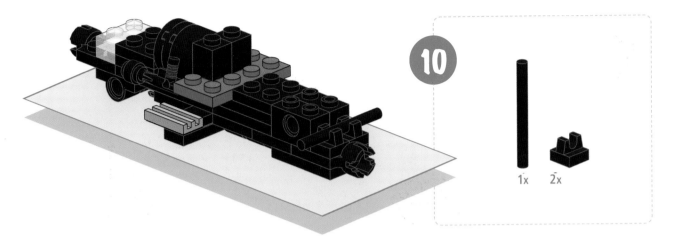

10

1x 2x

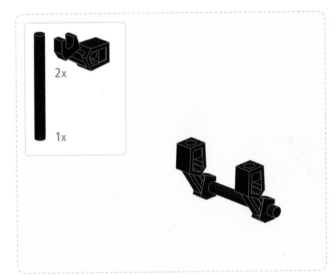

2x

1x

2x

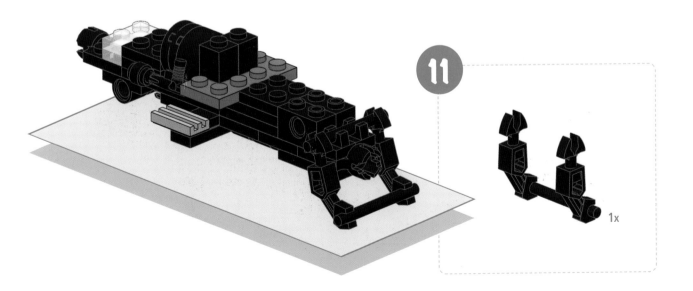

11

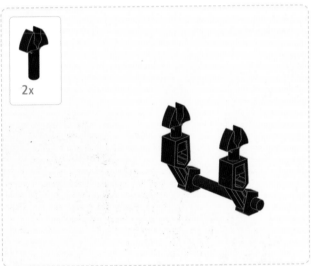

1x

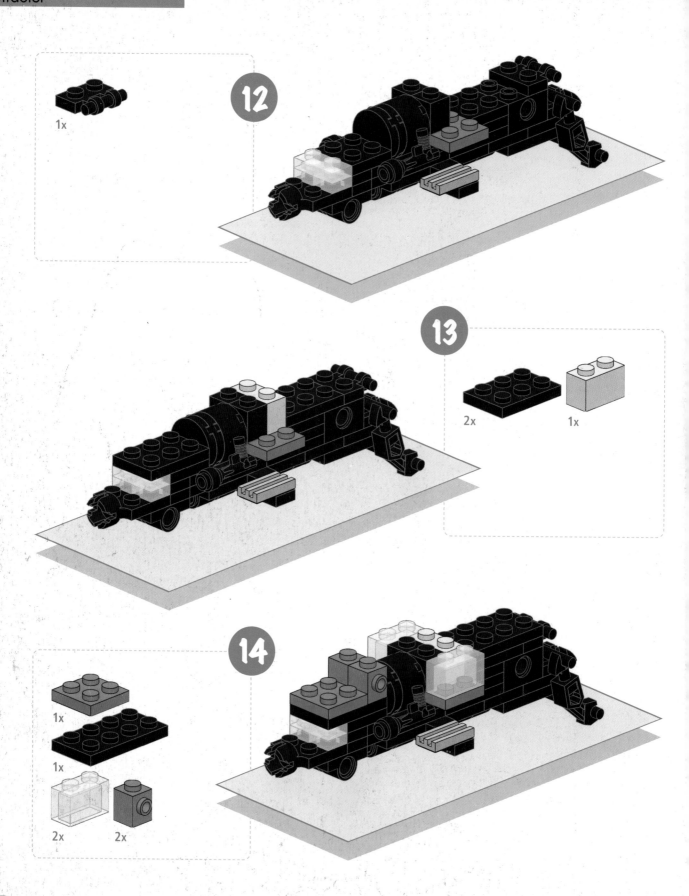

1x

12

13

2x   1x

14

1x

1x

2x   2x

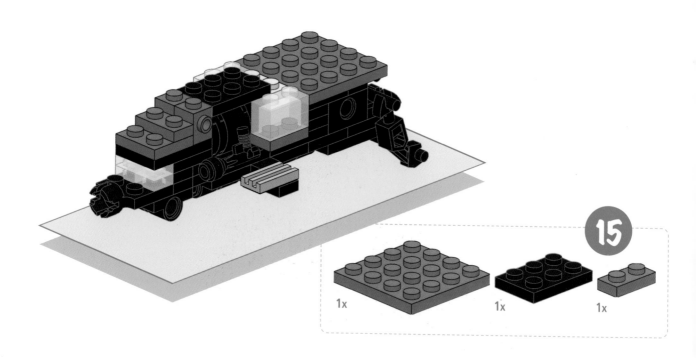

15

1x   1x   1x

After the photo shoot,
I had this idea for
improving the cockpit:
two more transparent
brick in the foot room.

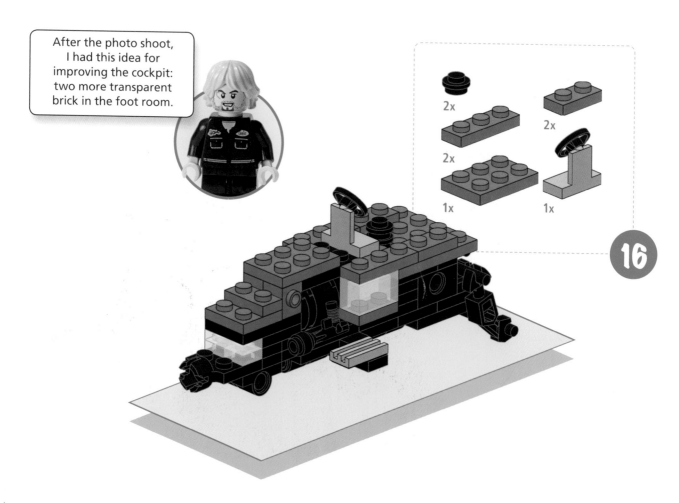

2x

2x

2x

1x   1x

16

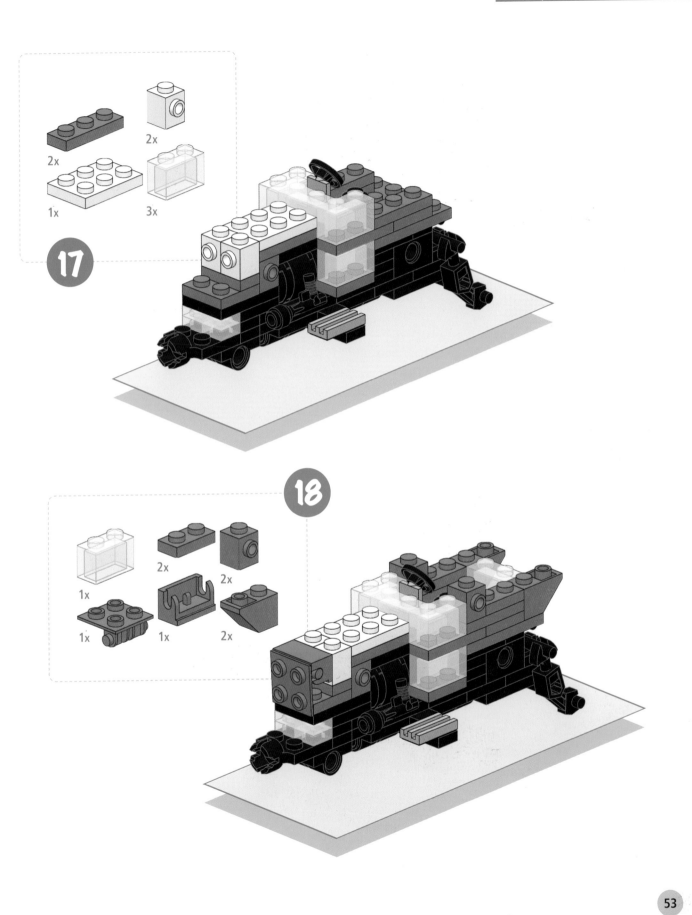

2x

2x

1x

3x

17

18

1x

2x

2x

1x

1x

2x

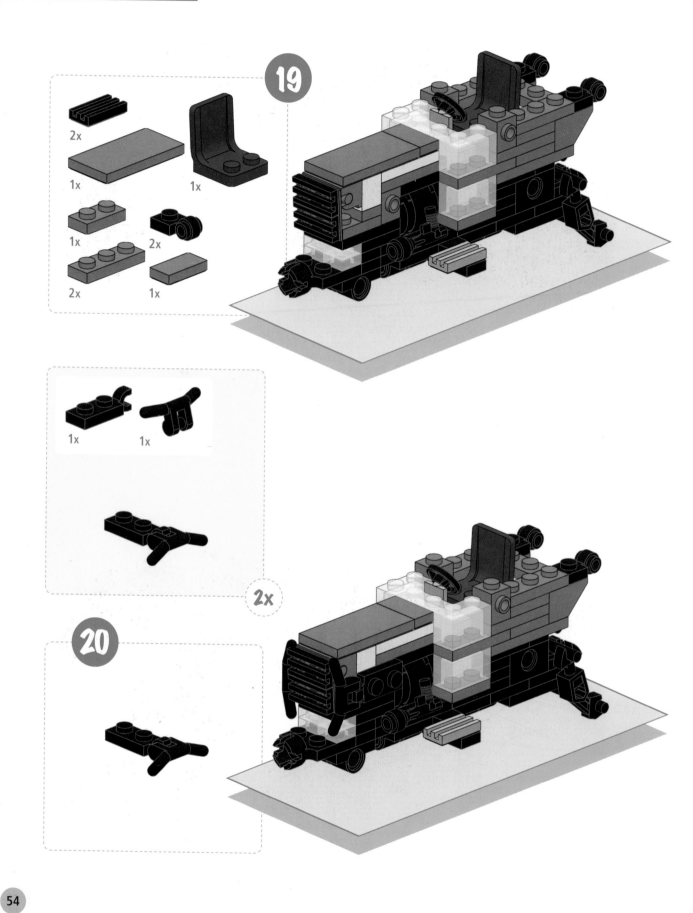

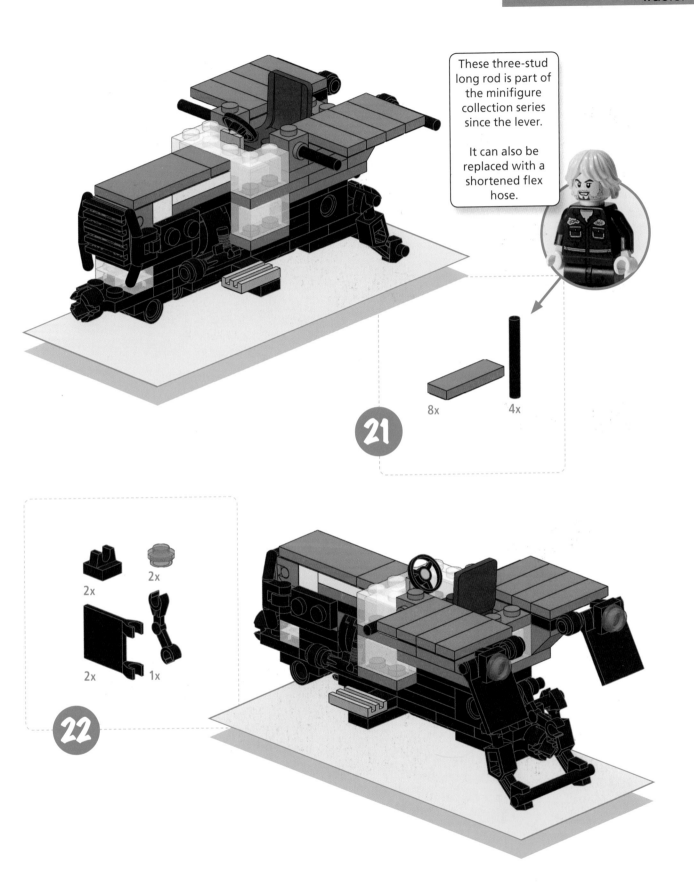

These three-stud long rod is part of the minifigure collection series since the lever.

It can also be replaced with a shortened flex hose.

8x   4x

21

2x   2x

2x   1x

22

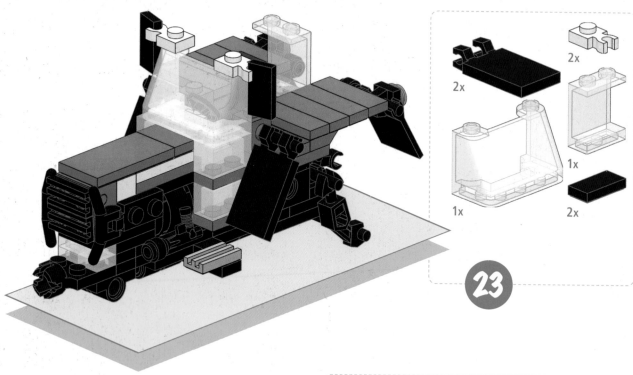

23

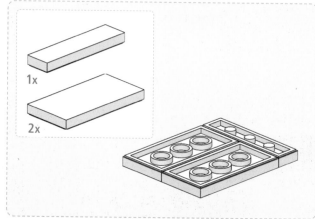

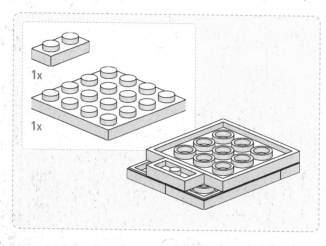

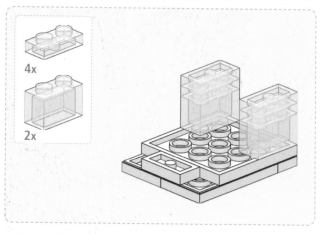

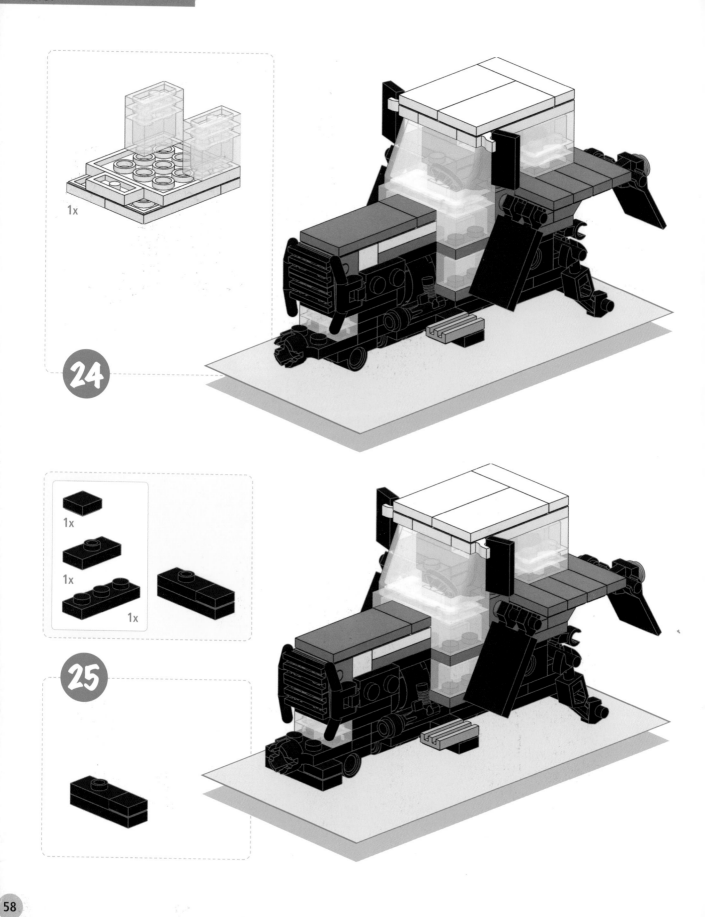

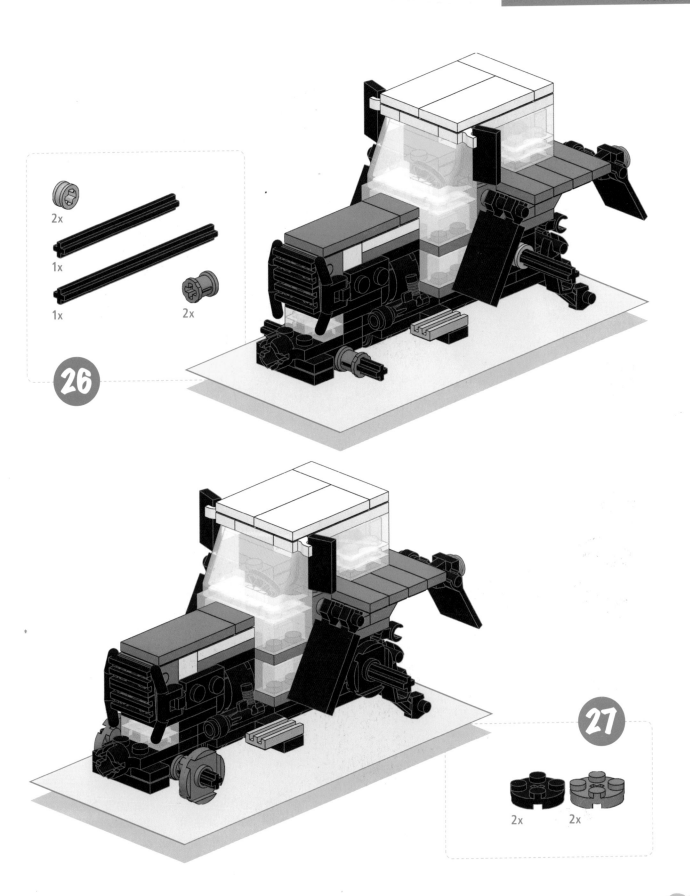

26

2x
1x
1x
2x

27

2x 2x

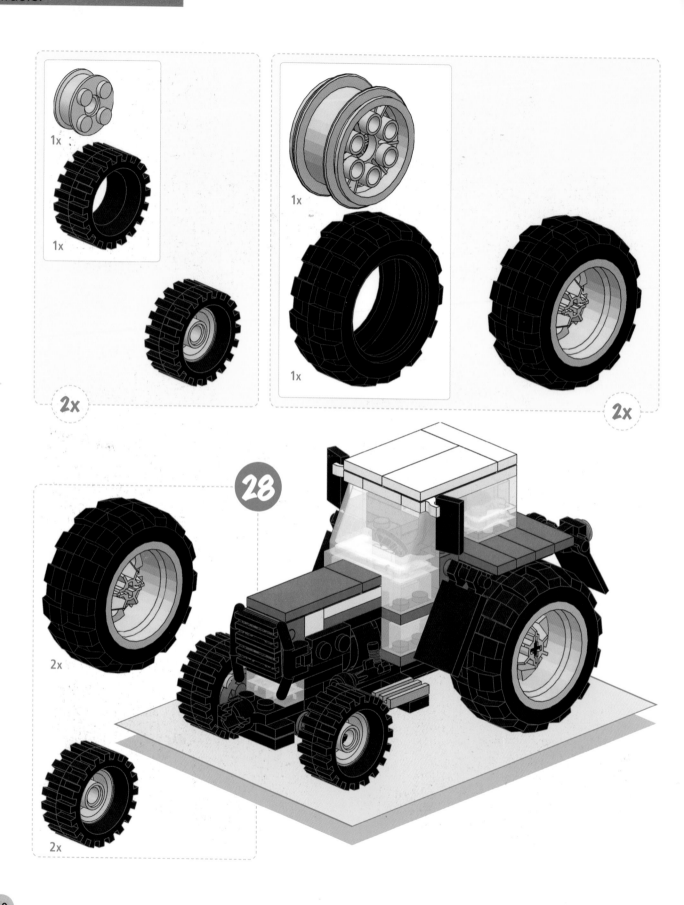

1x
1x
2x

1x

1x
2x

28

2x

2x

Parts List

2x

2x

2x

1x

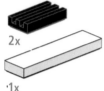
1x

1x

4x

1x

3x

2x

1x

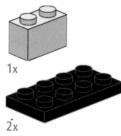
2x

5x

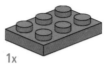
1x

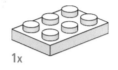
1x

2x

1x

3x

6x

4x

1x

4x

2x

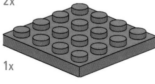
1x

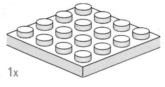
1x

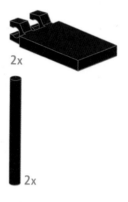
2x

2x

1x

8x

2x

1x

2x

2x

2x

2x

6

8

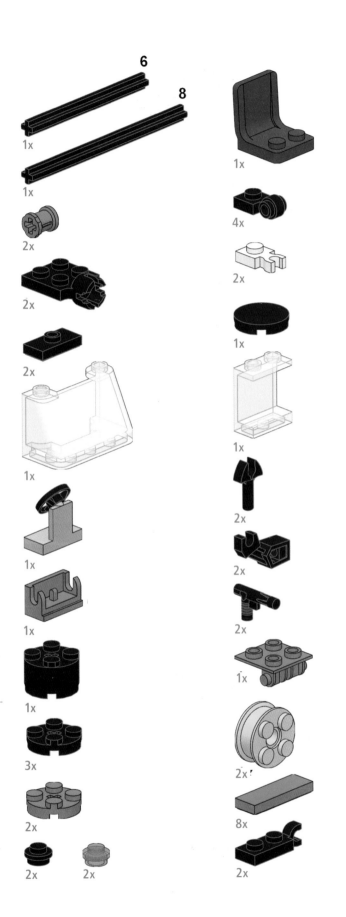

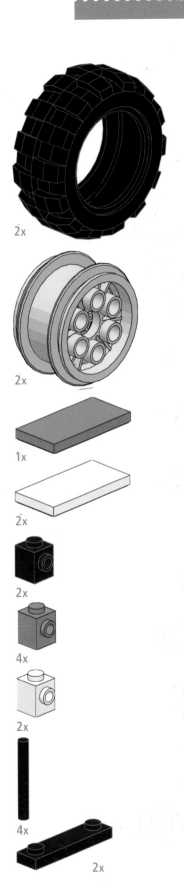

1x

1x

2x

2x

2x

1x

1x

1x

1x

3x

2x

2x   2x

1x

4x

2x

1x

1x

2x

2x

2x

1x

2x

8x

2x

2x

2x

1x

2x

1x

2x

2x

4x

2x

4x

2x

Quantity		Color	Element	Element Name
2		Black	2335	Flag 2 x 2
2		Black	2346	Tyre 12/ 50 x 16 Offset Tread
2		Black	2412b	Tile 1 x 2 Grille with Groove
1		White	2431	Tile 1 x 4 with Groove
1		Black	2444	Plate 2 x 2 with Hole
1		Black	2540	Plate 1 x 2 with Handle
4		Black	2555	Tile 1 x 1 with Clip
1		Black	2780	Technic Pin with Friction and Slots
3		Black	2817	Plate 2 x 2 with Holes
2		Black	30031	Minifig Handlebars
1		Tan	3004	Brick 1 x 2
2		Black	3020	Plate 2 x 4
5		Black	3021	Plate 2 x 3
1		Red	3021	Plate 2 x 3
1		White	3021	Plate 2 x 3
2		Black	3022	Plate 2 x 2
1		Red	3022	Plate 2 x 2
3		Black	3023	Plate 1 x 2
6		Red	3023	Plate 1 x 2
4		Trans-Clear	3023	Plate 1 x 2
1		White	3023	Plate 1 x 2
4		Trans-White	3024	Plate 1 x 1
2		Metallic Silver	30244	Tile 1 x 2 Grille with Groove
1		Red	3031	Plate 4 x 4
1		White	3031	Plate 4 x 4
2		Black	30350	Tile 2 x 3 with Horizontal Clips
2		Black	30374	Bar 4L Light Sabre Blade
1		Black	30377	Minifig Mechanical Arm
8		Trans-Clear	3065	Brick 1 x 2 without Centre Stud
2		Black	3069b	Tile 1 x 2 with Groove
1		Red	3069b	Tile 1 x 2 with Groove
2		Black	3070b	Tile 1 x 1 with Groove
2		Light Bluish Gray	32123a	Technic Bush 1/2 Smooth with Axle Hole Reduced
2		Black	3623	Plate 1 x 3
2		Red	3665	Slope Brick 45 2 x 1 Inverted

2		Black	3700	Technic Brick 1 x 2 with Hole
1		Black	3706	Technic Axle 6
1		Black	3707	Technic Axle 8
2		Red	3713	Technic Bush
2		Black	3730	Plate 2 x 2 with Towball Socket
2		Black	3794a	Plate 1 x 2 without Groove with 1 Centre Stud
1		Trans-Clear	3823	Windscreen 2 x 4 x 2
1		Light Bluish Gray	3829c01	Car Steering Stand and Wheel (Complete)
1		Red	3937	Hinge 1 x 2 Base
1		Black	3941	Brick 2 x 2 Round
3		Black	4032a	Plate 2 x 2 Round with Axlehole Type 1
2		Red	4032a	Plate 2 x 2 Round with Axlehole Type 1
2		Black	4073	Plate 1 x 1 Round
2		Trans-Red	4073	Plate 1 x 1 Round
1		Reddish Brown	4079	Minifig Seat 2 x 2
4		Black	4081b	Plate 1 x 1 with Clip Light Type 2
2		White	4085c	Plate 1 x 1 with Clip Vertical Type 3
1		Black	4150	Tile 2 x 2 Round
1		Trans-Clear	4864b	Panel 1 x 2 x 2 with Hollow Studs
2		Black	48729	Bar 1.5L with Clip
2		Black	53989	Minifig Mechanical Arm with Clip and Rod Hole
2		Black	58367	Minifig Hose Nozzle with Side String Hole
1		Red	6134	Hinge 2 x 2 Top
2		Yellow	6248	Wheel Basic with 4 Studs and Technic Peghole
8		Red	63864	Tile 1 x 3 with Groove
2		Black	63868	Plate 1 x 2 with Clip Horizontal on End
2		Black	6581	Tyre 20 x 30 Balloon Medium
2		Yellow	6582	Wheel 20 x 30 Balloon Medium
1		Red	87079	Tile 2 x 4 with Groove
2		White	87079	Tile 2 x 4 with Groove
2		Black	87087	Brick 1 x 1 with Stud on 1 Side
4		Red	87087	Brick 1 x 1 with Stud on 1 Side
2		White	87087	Brick 1 x 1 with Stud on 1 Side
4		Black	87994	Bar 3L
2		Black	92593	Plate 1 x 4 with Two Studs
1		Red	3020	Plate 2 x 4
6		Red	3623	Plate 1 x 3

Pick-up

I have steadily developed this model over time as well. At the beginning, when this small truck was very delicate and unremarkable, it was very important to me that the wheels turned. The printed 1x4 wooden tiles look really great on the truck bed. Naturally, you can also use brown, beige or black 1x8 tiles. As always, vary as you please.

As a special feature, this time we have created a rusted body as a guide, but solid color cars are also possible. All you need to do is replace the brown, dark orange and gray elements.

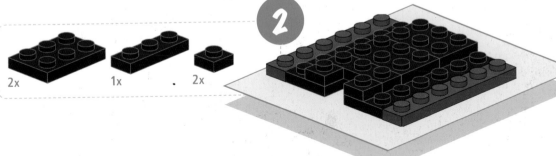

2x

2x

1

2x

1x

2x

2

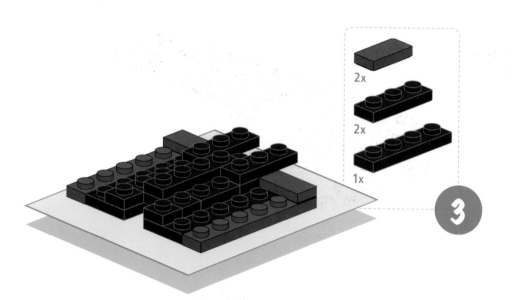

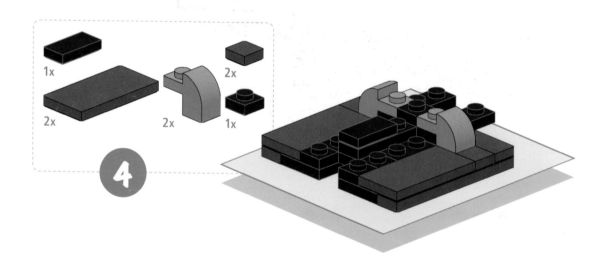

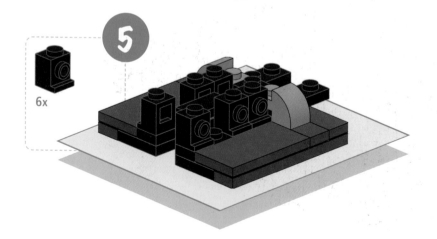

A single-color pick-up looks good, too, but this version with rust spots is more sophisticated.

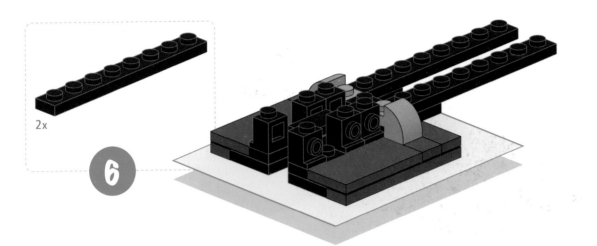

2x

6

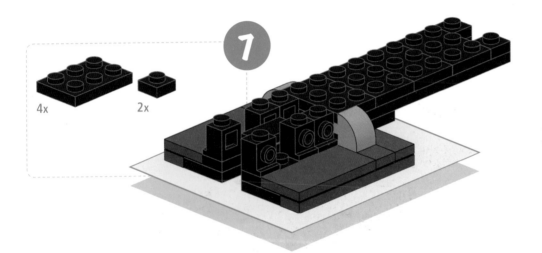

4x   2x

7

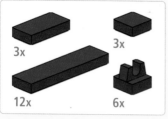

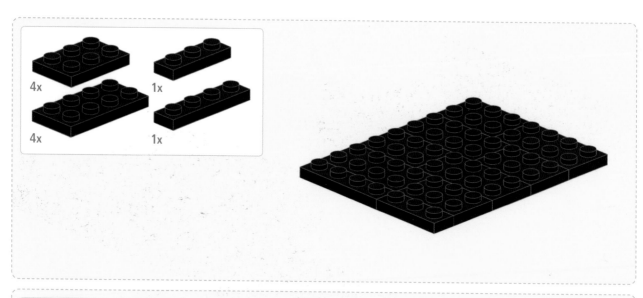

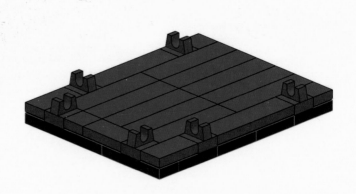

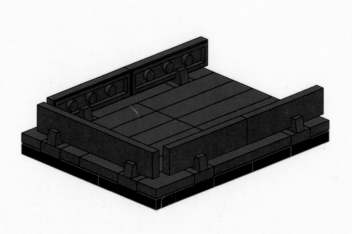

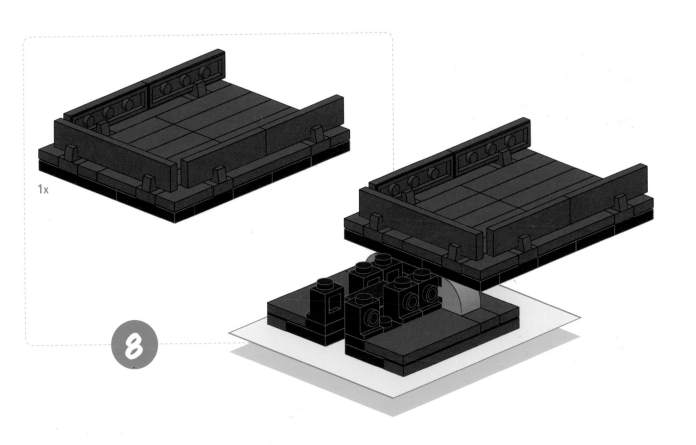

8

1x

1x   2x

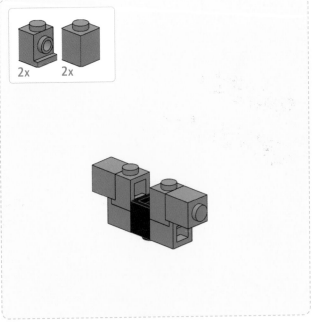

2x   2x

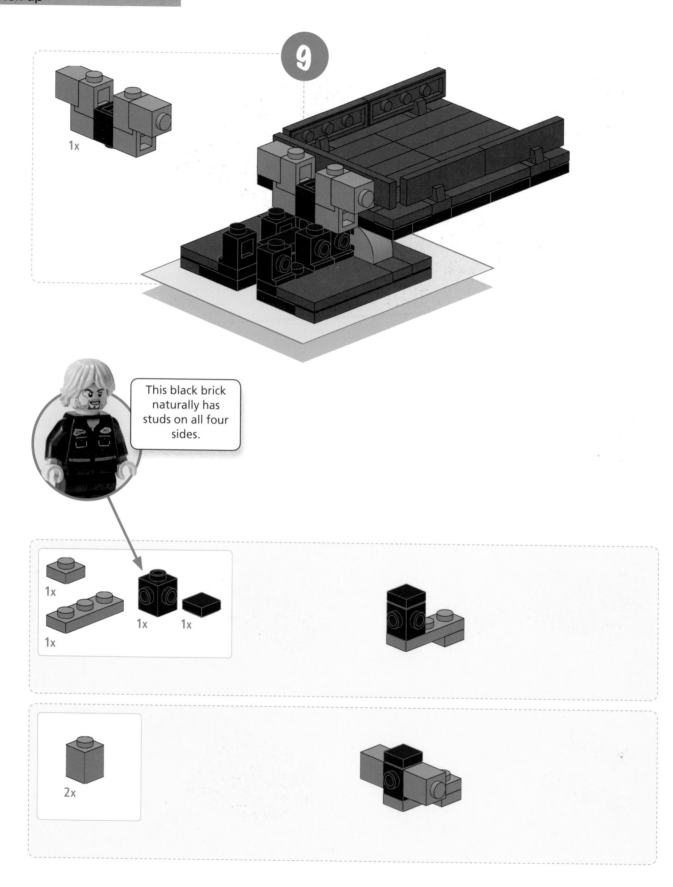

9

1x

This black brick
naturally has
studs on all four
sides.

1x

1x

1x

1x

2x

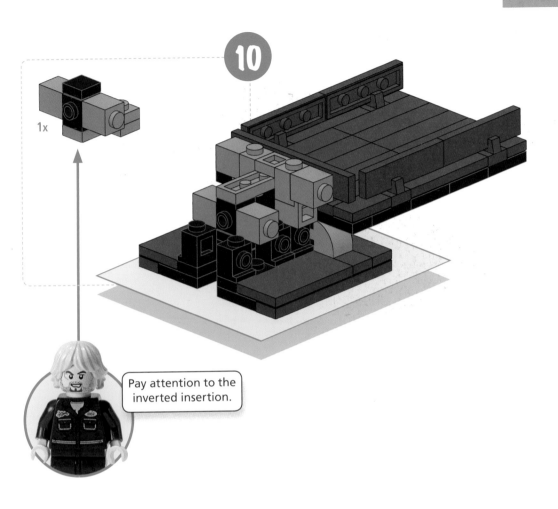

10

1x

Pay attention to the inverted insertion.

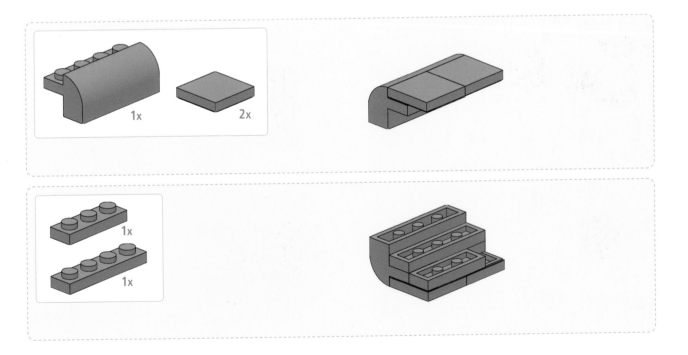

1x   2x

1x

1x

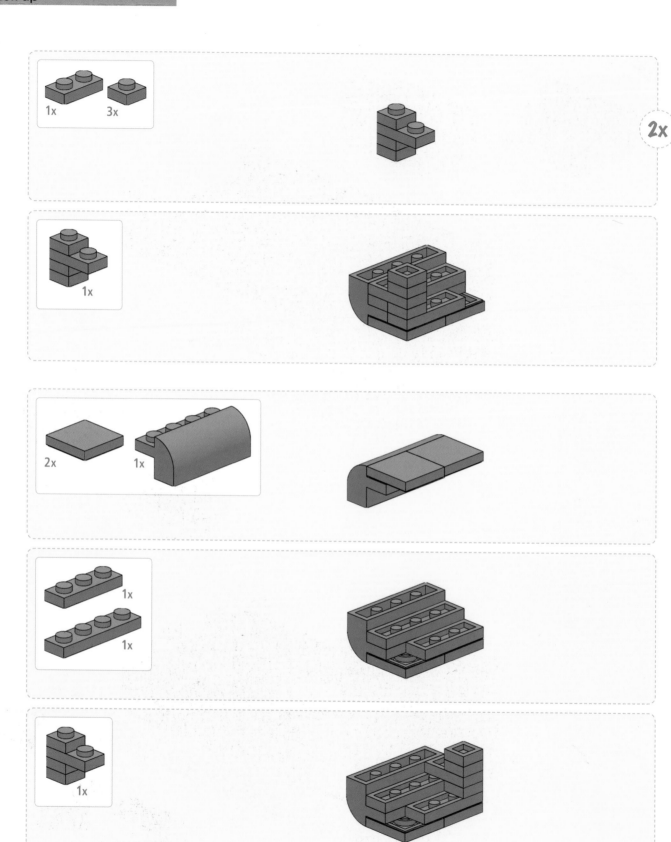

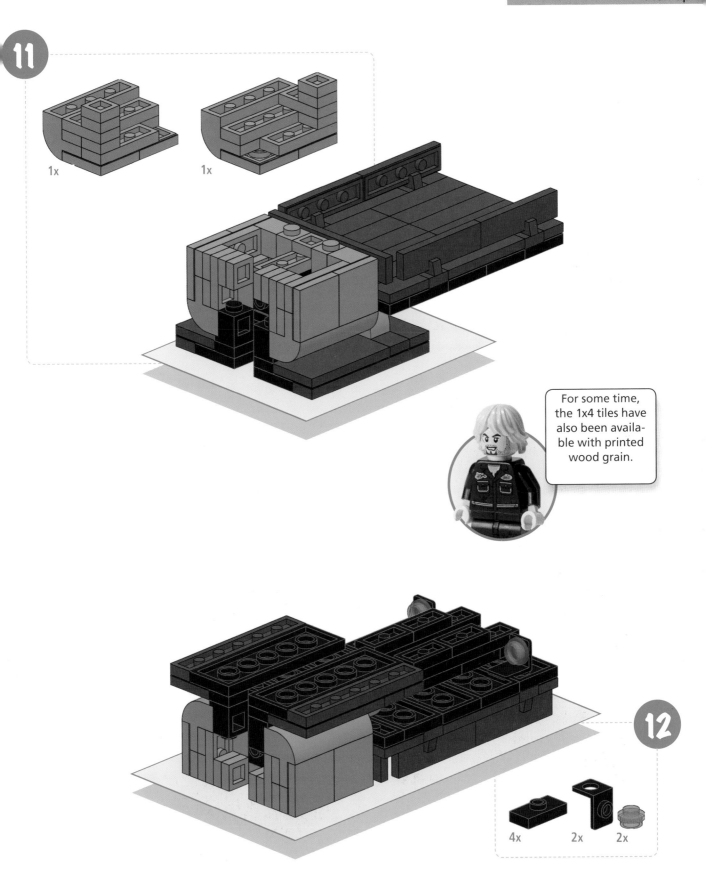

For some time, the 1x4 tiles have also been available with printed wood grain.

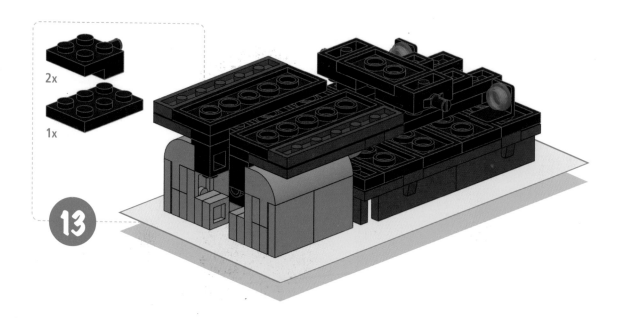

13

2x

1x

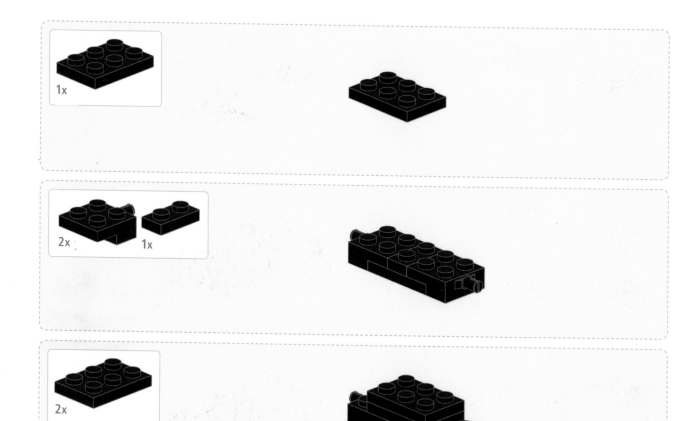

1x

2x 1x

2x

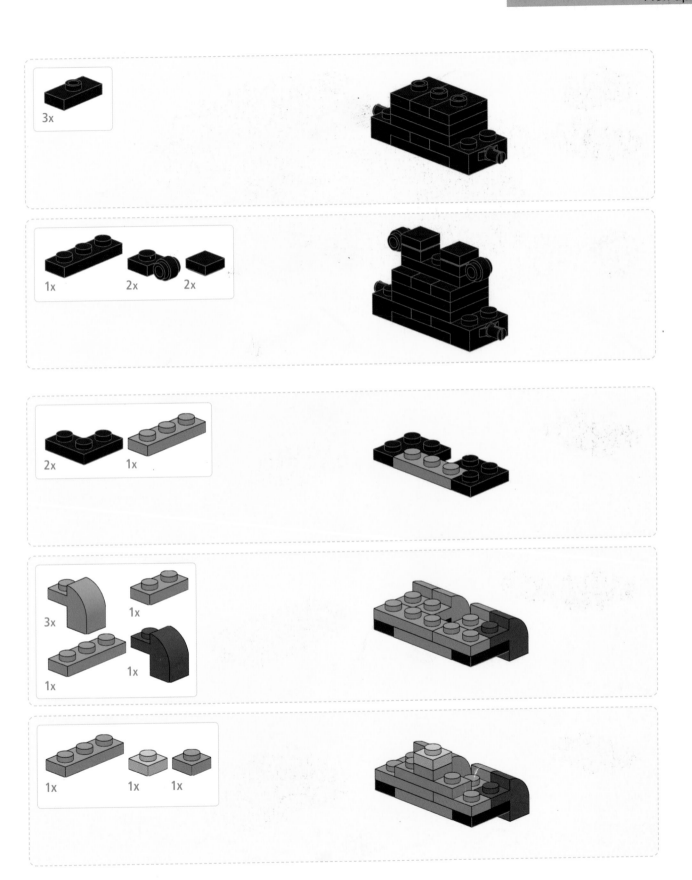

3x

1x **2x** **2x**

2x **1x**

3x **1x**

1x **1x**

1x **1x** **1x**

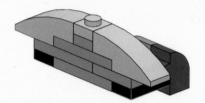

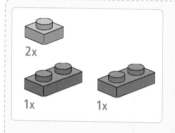

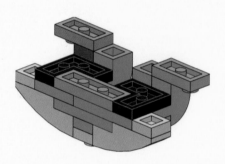

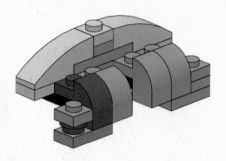

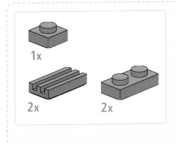

1x

2x 2x

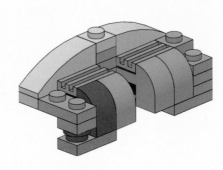

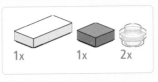

1x 1x 2x

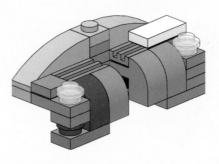

XFVXB8GT

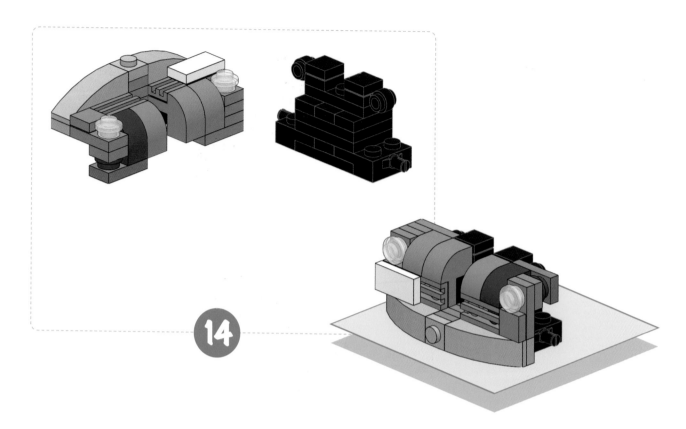

14

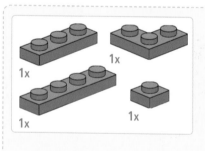

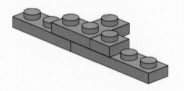

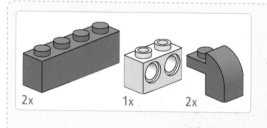

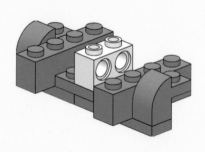

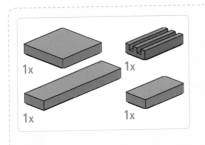

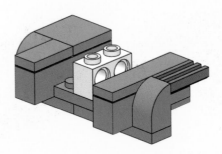

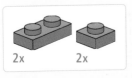

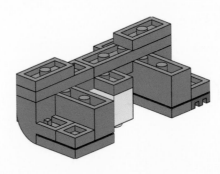

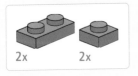

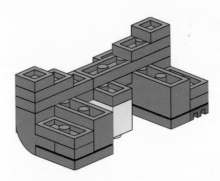

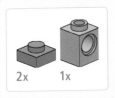

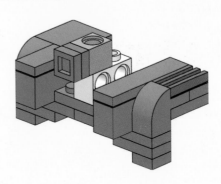

15

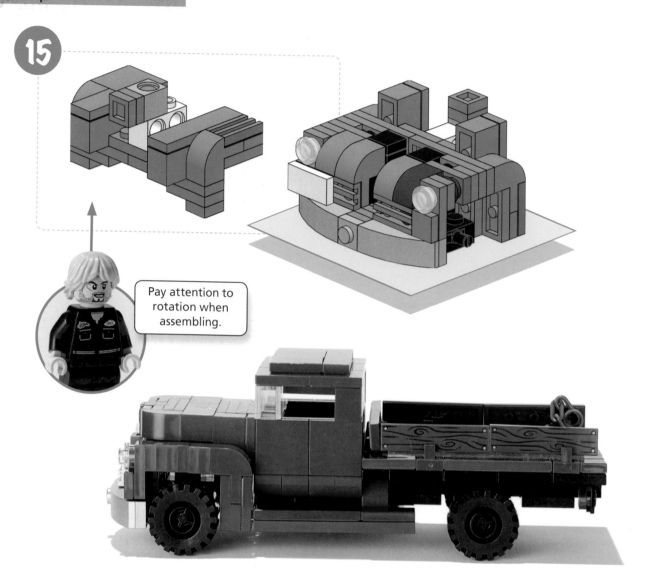

Pay attention to rotation when assembling.

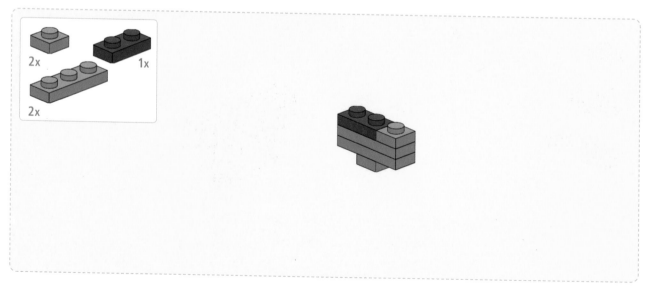

2x

1x

2x

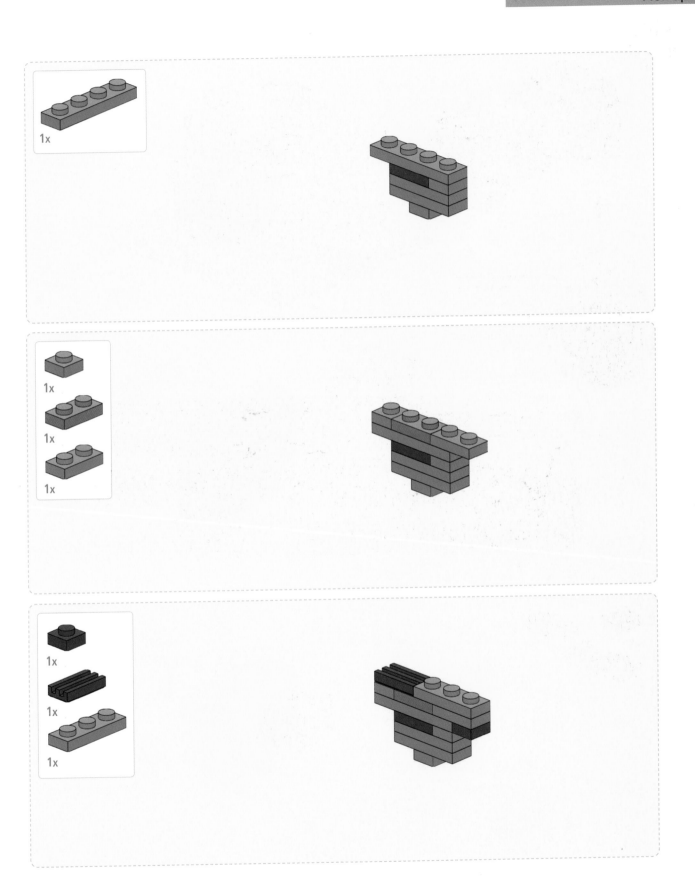

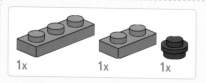

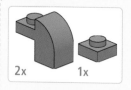

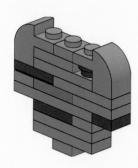

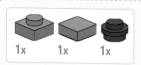

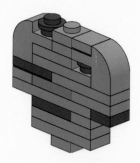

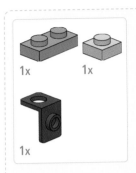

1x 1x

1x

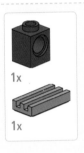

1x

1x

1x

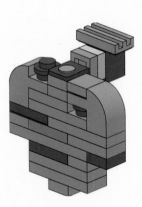

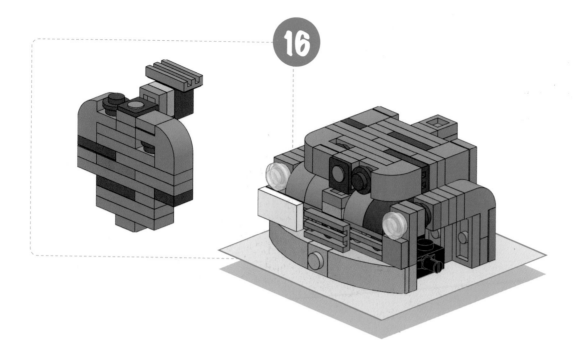

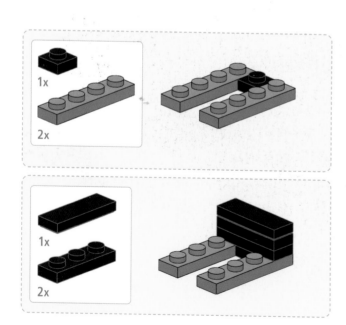

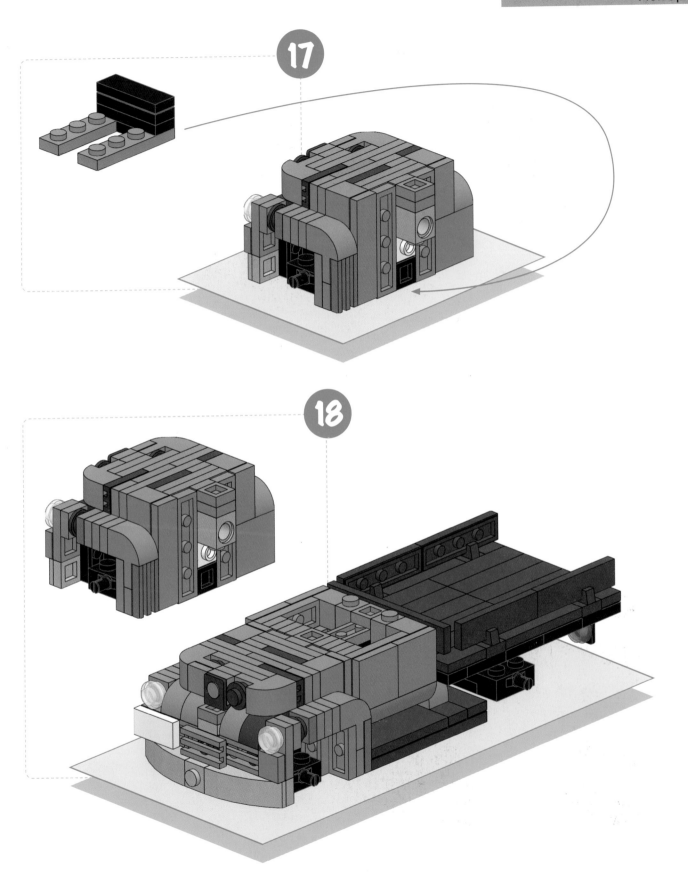

1x   1x

4x

4x

19

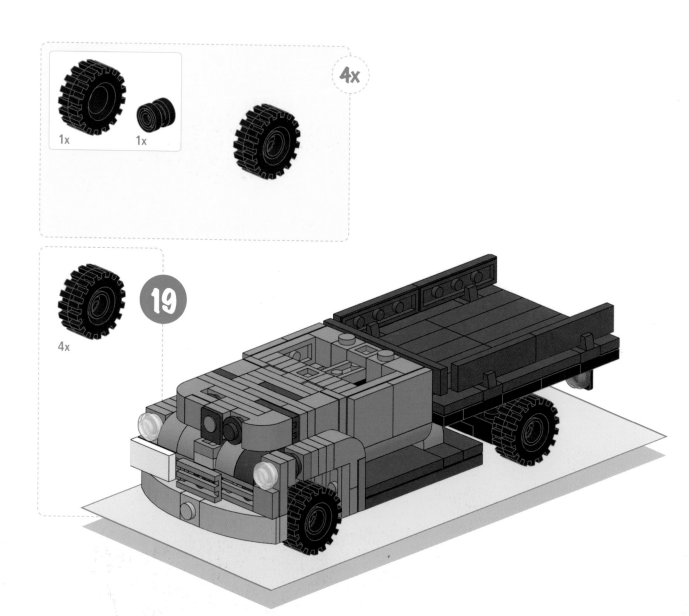

1x

1x

4x

1x

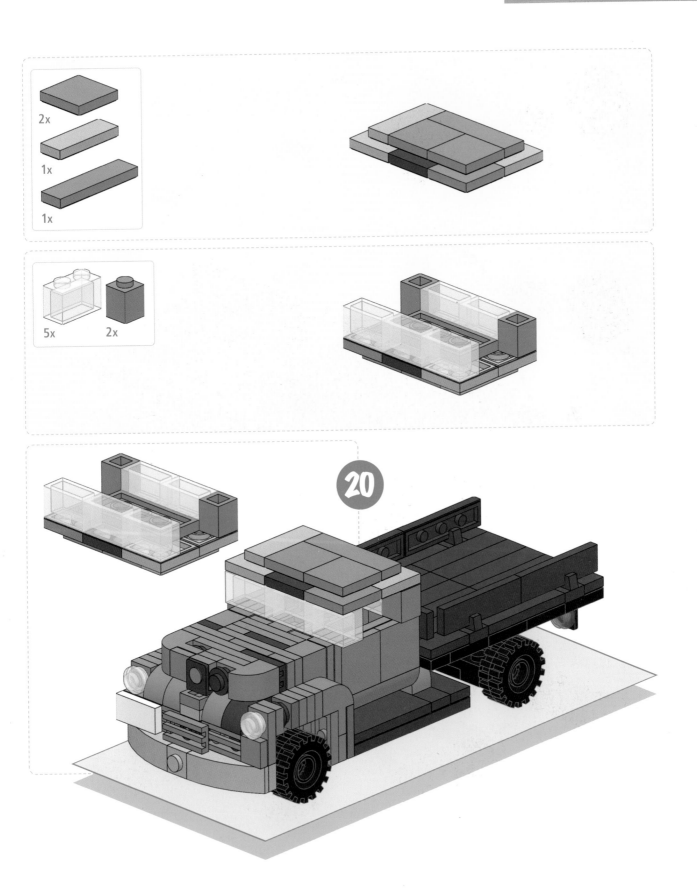

2x

1x

1x

5x   **2x**

20

Parts List

2x

1x

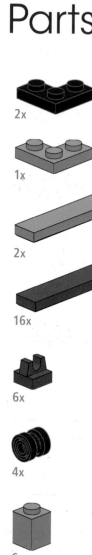
2x

16x

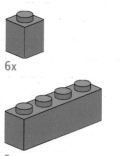
6x

4x

6x

2x

4x

1x

14x

1x

2x

13x

6x

24x

4x

1x

1x

3x

1x

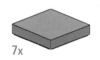
7x

1x

1x

5x

1x

3x

2x

5x

1x

2x

2x

2x

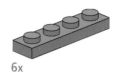
6x

7x

2x

6x

3x

2x

2x

2x

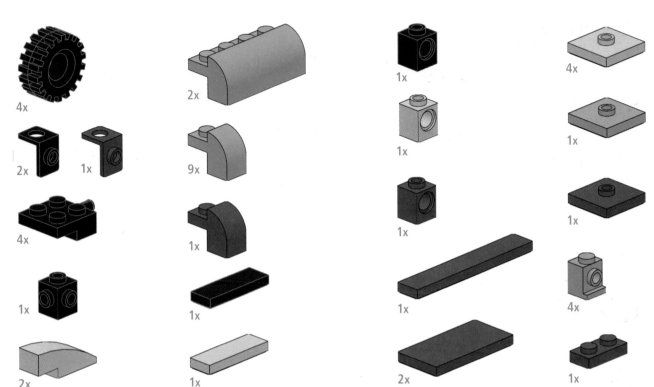

Quantity	Color	Element	Element Name
2	Black	2420	Plate 2 x 2 Corner
1	Medium Blue	2420	Plate 2 x 2 Corner
2	Medium Blue	2431	Tile 1 x 4 with Groove
16	Reddish Brown	2431	Tile 1 x 4 with Groove
6	Reddish Brown	2555	Tile 1 x 1 with Clip
4	Black	30027	Wheel Centre Small Wide for Slick Tyre
6	Medium Blue	3005	Brick 1 x 1
2	Medium Blue	3010	Brick 1 x 4
4	Black	3020	Plate 2 x 4
1	Medium Blue	3020	Plate 2 x 4
14	Black	3021	Plate 2 x 3
1	Black	3023	Plate 1 x 2
2	Dark Orange	3023	Plate 1 x 2
13	Medium Blue	3023	Plate 1 x 2
6	Black	3024	Plate 1 x 1
24	Medium Blue	3024	Plate 1 x 1
4	Metallic Silver	3024	Plate 1 x 1
1	Reddish Brown	3024	Plate 1 x 1
1	Dark Orange	30244	Tile 1 x 2 Grille with Groove
3	Medium Blue	30244	Tile 1 x 2 Grille with Groove
1	Reddish Brown	30244	Tile 1 x 2 Grille with Groove
5	Trans-Clear	3065	Brick 1 x 2 without Centre Stud

7	Medium Blue	3068b	Tile 2 x 2 with Groove
1	Black	3069b	Tile 1 x 2 with Groove
1	Medium Blue	3069b	Tile 1 x 2 with Groove
5	Reddish Brown	3069b	Tile 1 x 2 with Groove
1	White	3069b	Tile 1 x 2 with Groove
3	Black	3070b	Tile 1 x 1 with Groove
2	Medium Blue	3070b	Tile 1 x 1 with Groove
5	Reddish Brown	3070b	Tile 1 x 1 with Groove
1	White	32000	Technic Brick 1 x 2 with Holes
2	Black	3460	Plate 1 x 8
7	Black	3623	Plate 1 x 3
11	Medium Blue	3623	Plate 1 x 3
2	Reddish Brown	3666	Plate 1 x 6
2	Black	3710	Plate 1 x 4
6	Medium Blue	3710	Plate 1 x 4
7	Black	3794a	Plate 1 x 2 without Groove with 1 Centre Stud
2	Black	3795	Plate 2 x 6
6	Black	4070	Brick 1 x 1 with Headlight
3	Reddish Brown	4073	Plate 1 x 1 Round
2	Trans-Red	4073	Plate 1 x 1 Round
2	Trans-Clear	4073	Plate 1 x 1 Round
2	Black	4081b	Plate 1 x 1 with Clip Light Type 2
4	Black	4084	Tyre 8/ 75 x 8 Offset Tread
2	Black	42446	Bracket 1 x 1 - 1 x 1
1	Reddish Brown	42446	Bracket 1 x 1 - 1 x 1
4	Black	4488	Plate 2 x 2 with Wheel Holder
1	Black	4733	Brick 1 x 1 with Studs on Four Sides
2	Metallic Silver	50950	Slope Brick Curved 3 x 1
2	Medium Blue	6081	Brick 2 x 4 x 1 & 1/3 with Curved Top
9	Medium Blue	6091	Brick 2 x 1 x 1 & 1/3 with Curved Top
1	Reddish Brown	6091	Brick 2 x 1 x 1 & 1/3 with Curved Top
1	Black	63864	Tile 1 x 3 with Groove
1	Light Bluish Gray	63864	Tile 1 x 3 with Groove
1	Black	6541	Technic Brick 1 x 1 with Hole
1	Light Bluish Gray	6541	Technic Brick 1 x 1 with Hole
1	Reddish Brown	6541	Technic Brick 1 x 1 with Hole
1	Reddish Brown	6636	Tile 1 x 6
2	Reddish Brown	87079	Tile 2 x 4 with Groove
4	Light Bluish Gray	87580	Plate 2 x 2 with Groove with 1 Center Stud
1	Medium Blue	87580	Plate 2 x 2 with Groove with 1 Center Stud
1	Reddish Brown	87580	Plate 2 x 2 with Groove with 1 Center Stud
4	Medium Blue	4070	Brick 1 x 1 with Headlight
1	Reddish Brown	3023	Plate 1 x 2

Stool

Did you know that the "X" on the back-side of a 2x2 round tile fits exactly on the underside of a brick? This way, you can conjure up a stool with only a few elements.

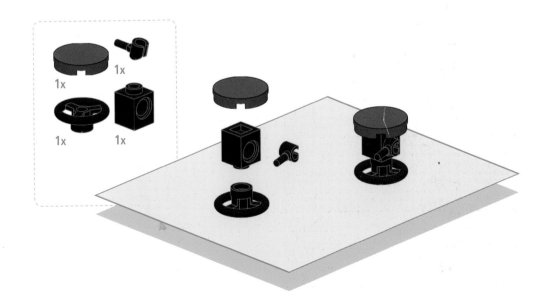

Classic car

And here it is…! By popular demand from many LEGO® fans—the blueprint for this classic car. As I explained in the foreword, this model is only for show in your cabinet or as a standing model; therefore, the wheels do not turn. It is possible to build it so that it rolls, but that will make the model very unsteady, because the stabilizing parts will have to be removed and/or replaced. Thus, we have decided to show the original version. Maybe you can find a better solution?

1

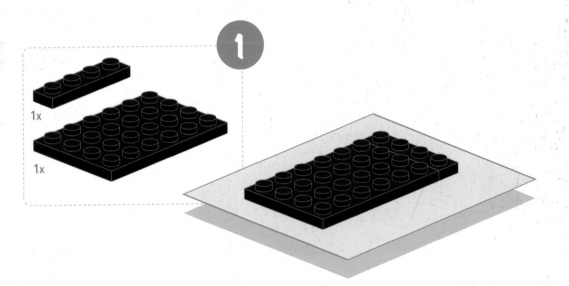

1x

1x

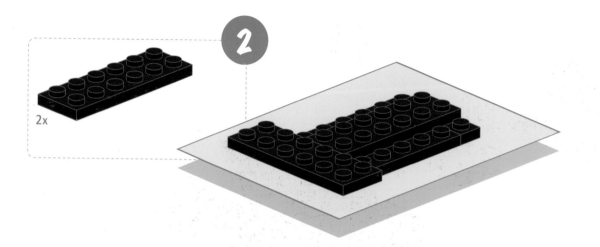

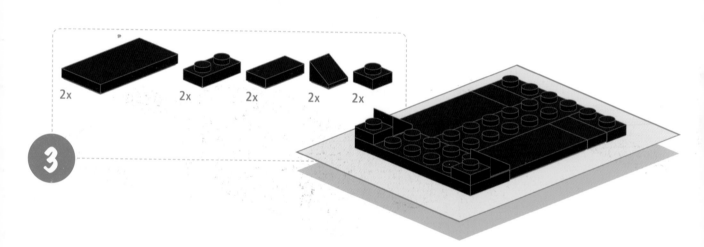

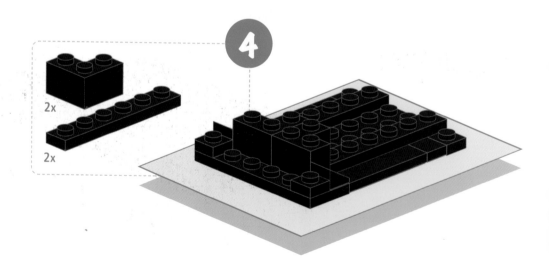

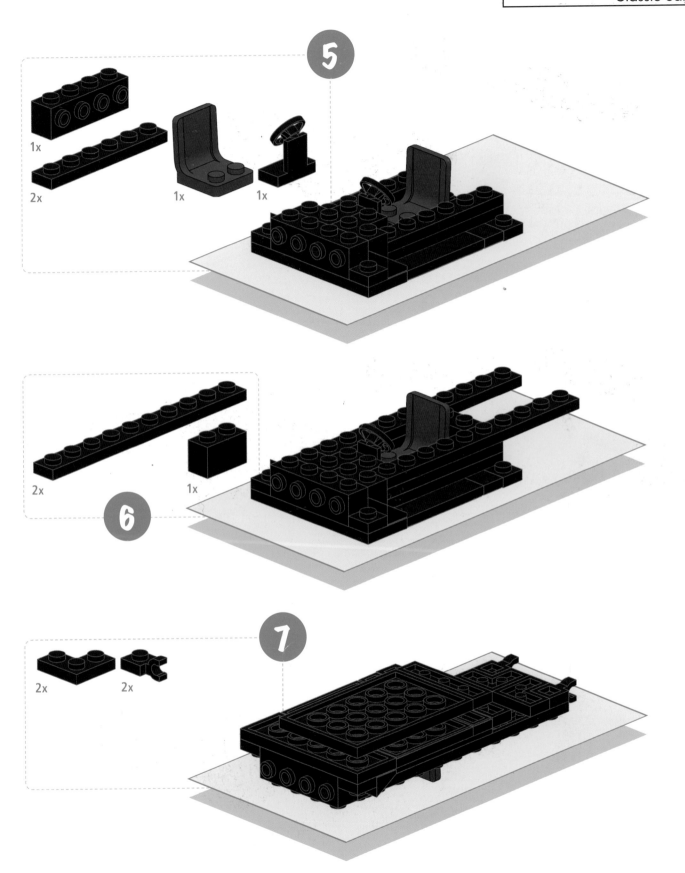

5

1x

2x

1x

1x

6

2x

1x

7

2x

2x

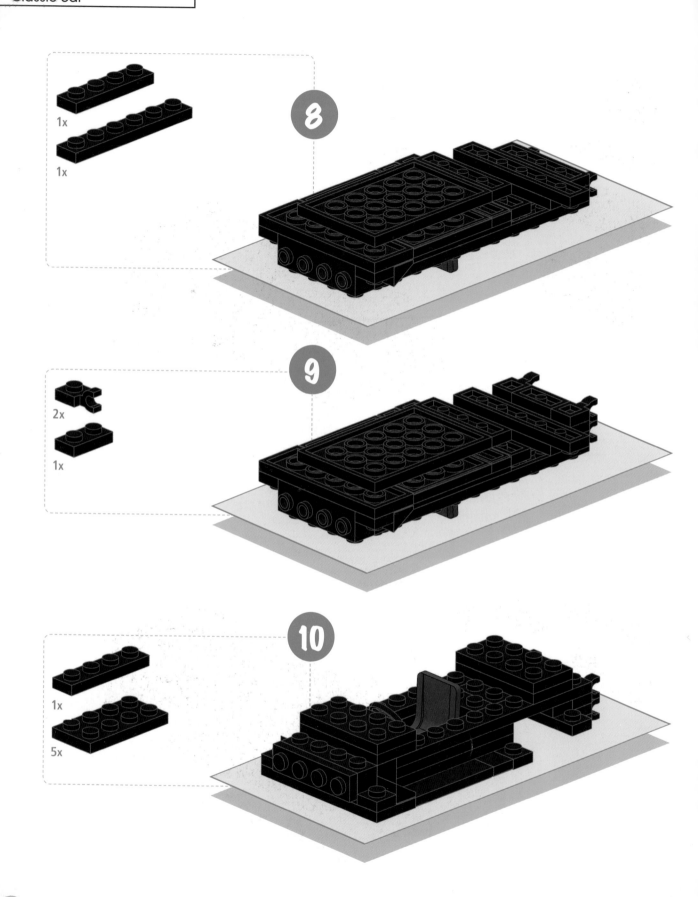

1x

1x

8

2x

1x

9

1x

5x

10

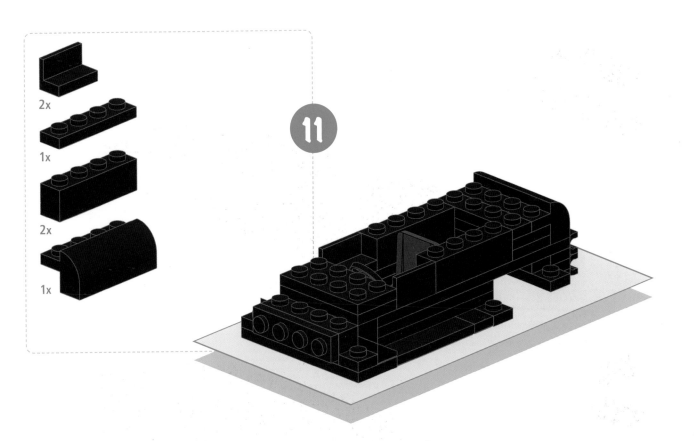

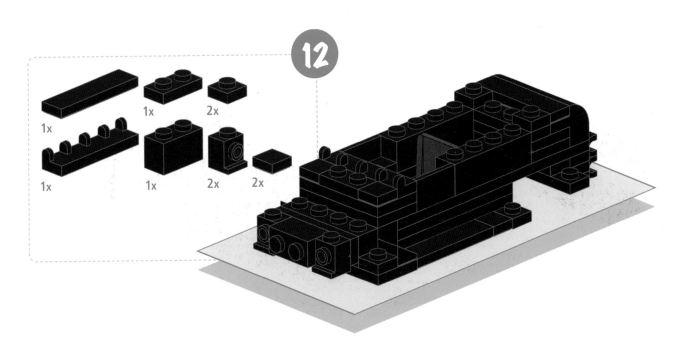

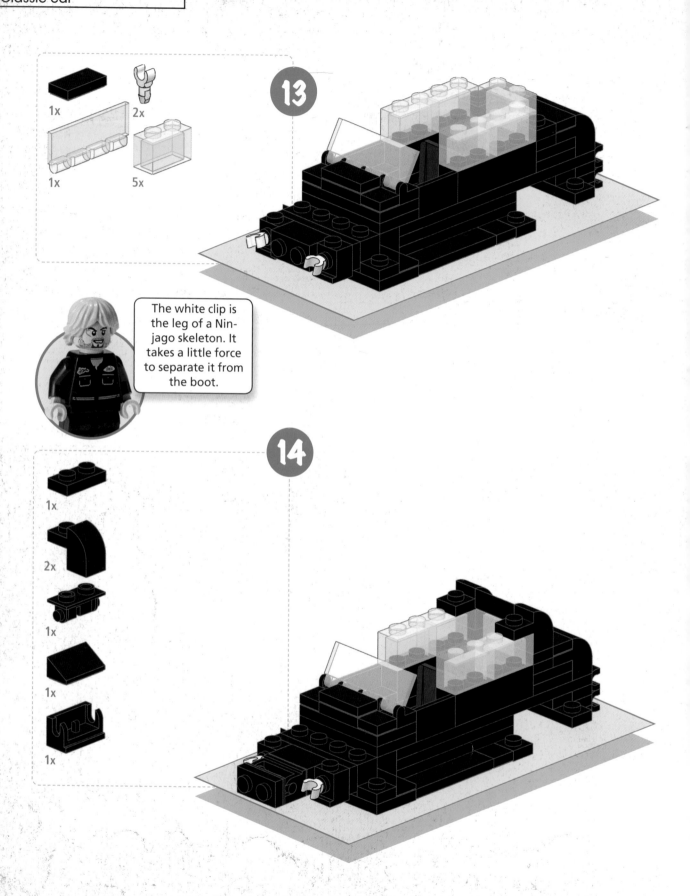

1x

2x

1x

5x

13

The white clip is the leg of a Ninjago skeleton. It takes a little force to separate it from the boot.

14

1x

2x

1x

1x

1x

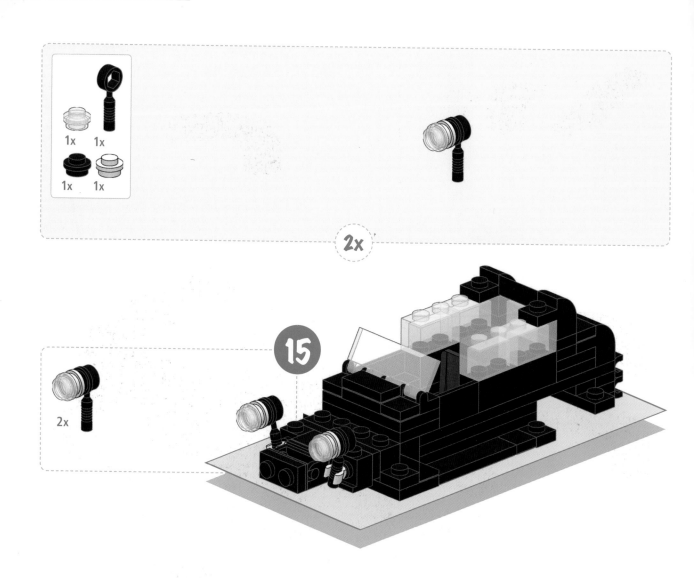

15

2x

2x

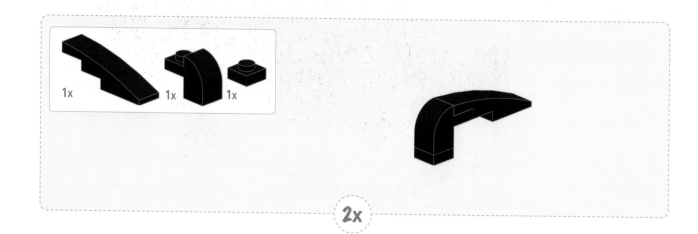

2x

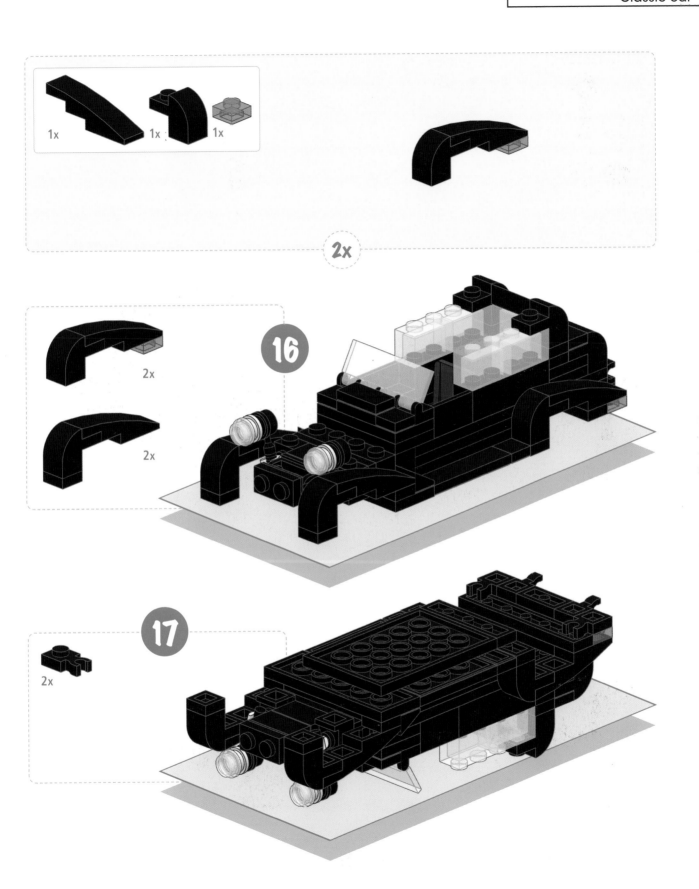

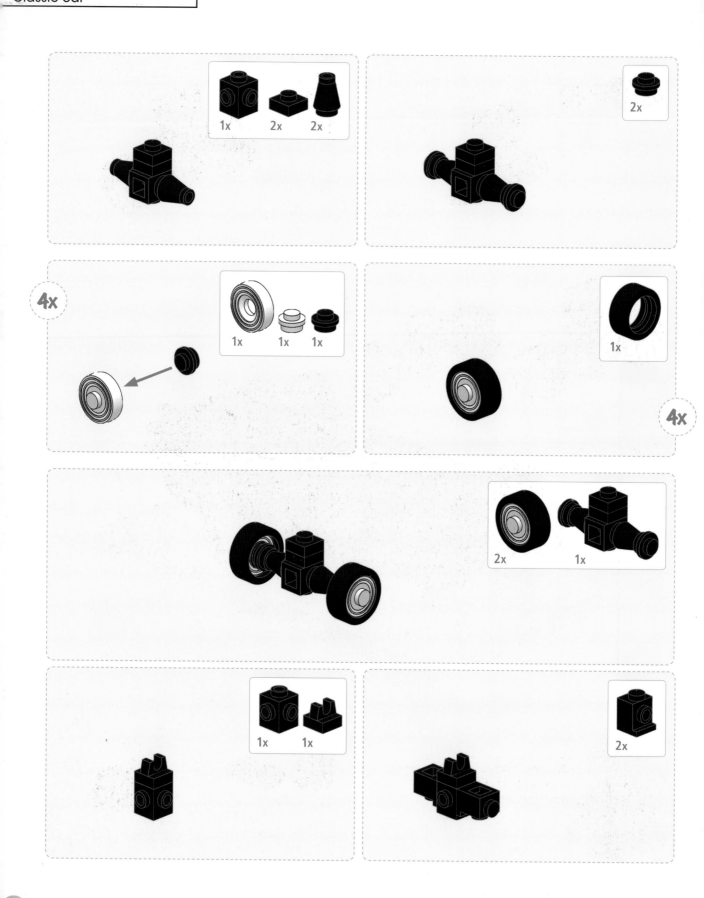

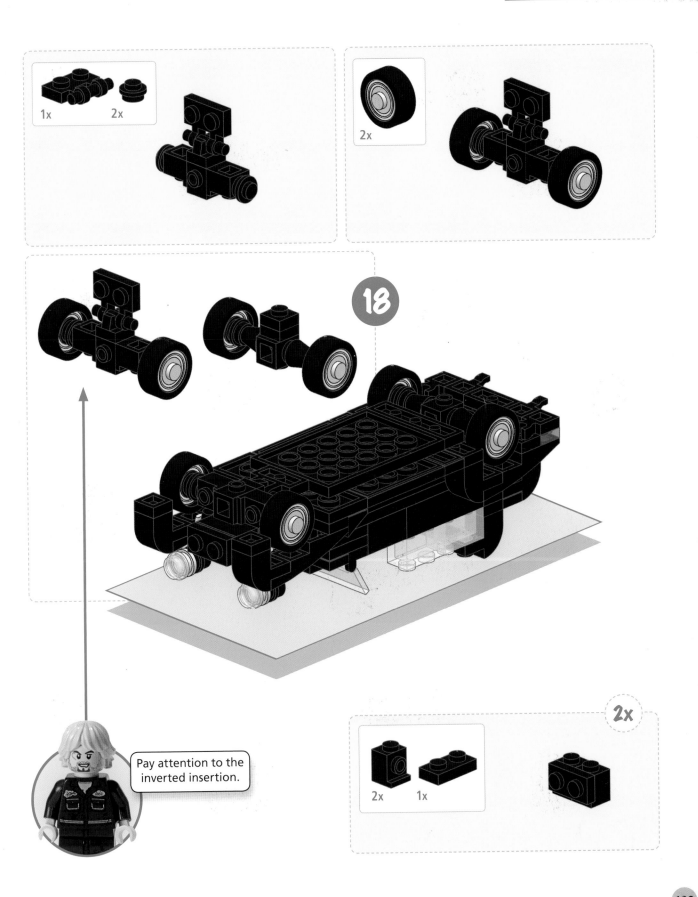

1x   2x

2x

18

2x

Pay attention to the
inverted insertion.

2x   1x

2x

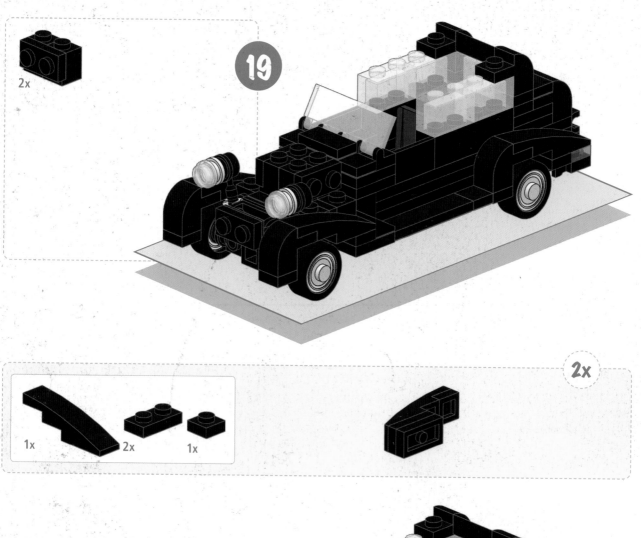

19

1x   2x   1x

2x

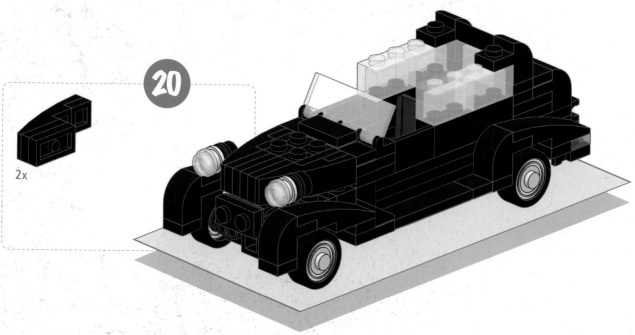

20

2x

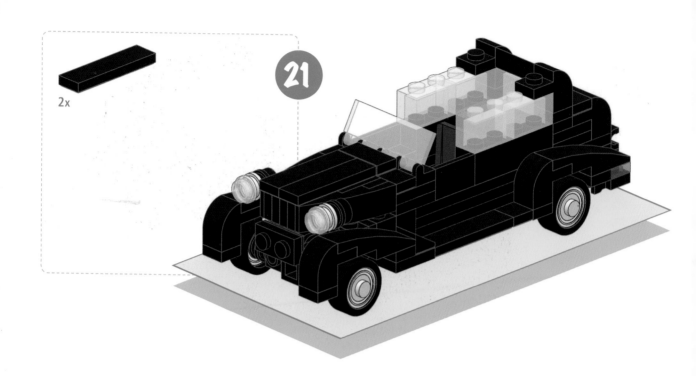

2x

21

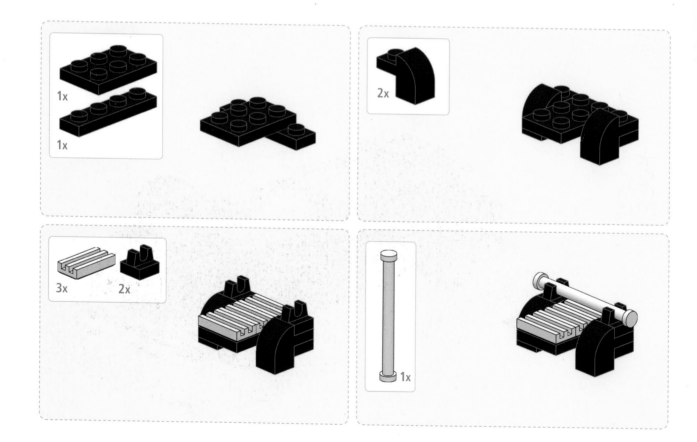

1x
1x

2x

3x   2x

1x

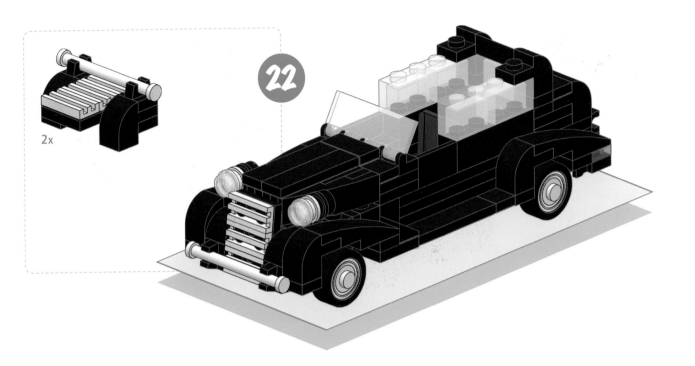

2x

22

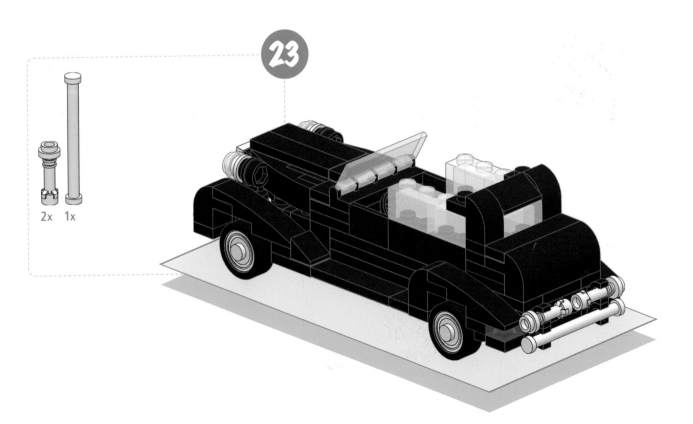

2x 1x

23

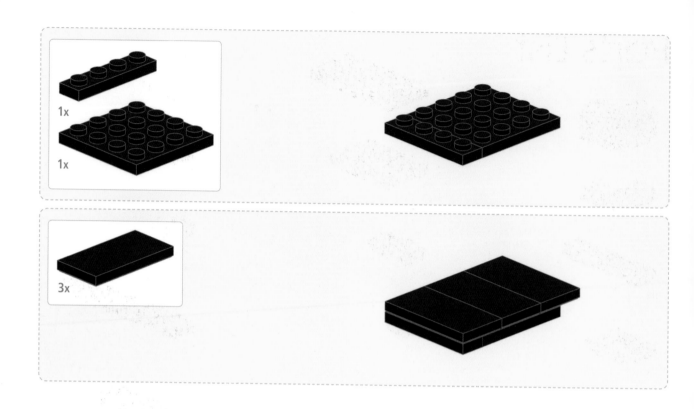

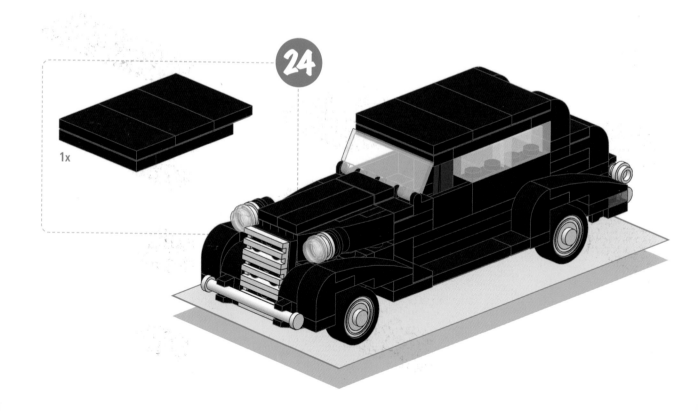

Parts List

2x

2x

3x

1x

3x

2x

2x

2x

1x

5x

1x

11x

10x

2x

3x

1x

1x

1x

5x

3x

4x

5x

6x

2x

1x

1x

1x

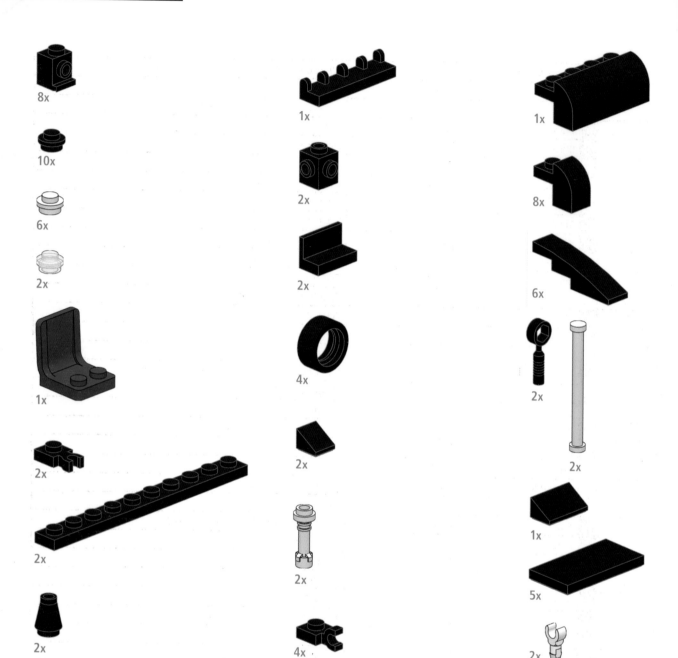

Quantity	Color		Element	Element Name
2		Black	2357	Brick 2 x 2 Corner
2		Black	2420	Plate 2 x 2 Corner
3		Black	2431	Tile 1 x 4 with Groove
1		Black	2540	Plate 1 x 2 with Handle
3		Black	2555	Tile 1 x 1 with Clip
2		Black	30039	Tile 1 x 1 with Groove
2		Black	3004	Brick 1 x 2
2		Black	3010	Brick 1 x 4

1	Trans-White	30161	Windscreen 1 x 4 x 1.3 Bottom Hinge
5	Black	3020	Plate 2 x 4
1	Black	3021	Plate 2 x 3
11	Black	3023	Plate 1 x 2
10	Black	3024	Plate 1 x 1
2	Trans-Red	3024	Plate 1 x 1
3	Chrome Silver	30244	Tile 1 x 2 Grille with Groove
1	Black	3031	Plate 4 x 4
1	Black	3032	Plate 4 x 6
1	Black	30414	Brick 1 x 4 with Studs on Side
5	Trans-Clear	3065	Brick 1 x 2 without Centre Stud
3	Black	3069b	Tile 1 x 2 with Groove
4	White	3139	Tyre 14 x 10 Single Smooth
5	Black	3666	Plate 1 x 6
6	Black	3710	Plate 1 x 4
2	Black	3795	Plate 2 x 6
1	Black	3829c01	Car Steering Stand and Wheel (Complete)
1	Black	3937	Hinge 1 x 2 Base
1	Black	3938	Hinge 1 x 2 Top
8	Black	4070	Brick 1 x 1 with Headlight
10	Black	4073	Plate 1 x 1 Round
6	Chrome Silver	4073	Plate 1 x 1 Round
2	Trans-Clear	4073	Plate 1 x 1 Round
1	Reddish Brown	4079	Minifig Seat 2 x 2
2	Black	4085c	Plate 1 x 1 with Clip Vertical Type 3
2	Black	4477	Plate 1 x 10
2	Black	4589	Cone 1 x 1
1	Black	4625	Hinge Tile 1 x 4
2	Black	4733	Brick 1 x 1 with Studs on Four Sides
2	Black	4865a	Panel 1 x 2 x 1 with Square Corners
4	Black	50951	Tyre 6/ 30 x 11
2	Black	54200	Slope Brick 31 1 x 1 x 2/3
2	Chrome Silver	577	Minifig Tool Light Sabre Hilt
4	Black	6019	Plate 1 x 1 with Clip Horizontal
1	Black	6081	Brick 2 x 4 x 1 & 1/3 with Curved Top
8	Black	6091	Brick 2 x 1 x 1 & 1/3 with Curved Top
6	Black	61678	Slope Brick Curved 4 x 1
2	Black	6246d	Minifig Tool Box Wrench
2	Chrome Silver	71184	Bar 4.5L Straight
1	Black	85984	Slope Brick 31 1 x 2 x 0.667
5	Black	87079	Tile 2 x 4 with Groove
2	White	93612	~Minifig Skeleton Leg with Black Square Foot, Leg

Parts tray

This tray for sorting and storing small parts is a good example of how you can achieve amazing results in simple ways. Simply build up colored bricks behind the transparent bricks; the combination will make the compartments look filled.

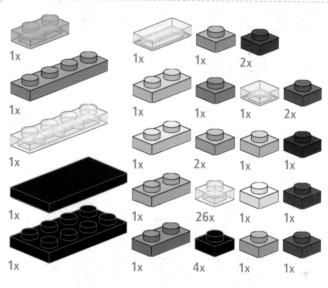

1x	1x	1x	2x
1x	1x	1x	2x
1x	1x	2x	1x	1x
1x	1x	26x	1x	1x
1x	1x	4x	1x	1x

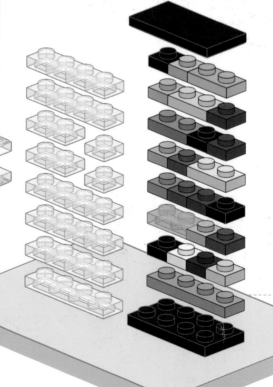

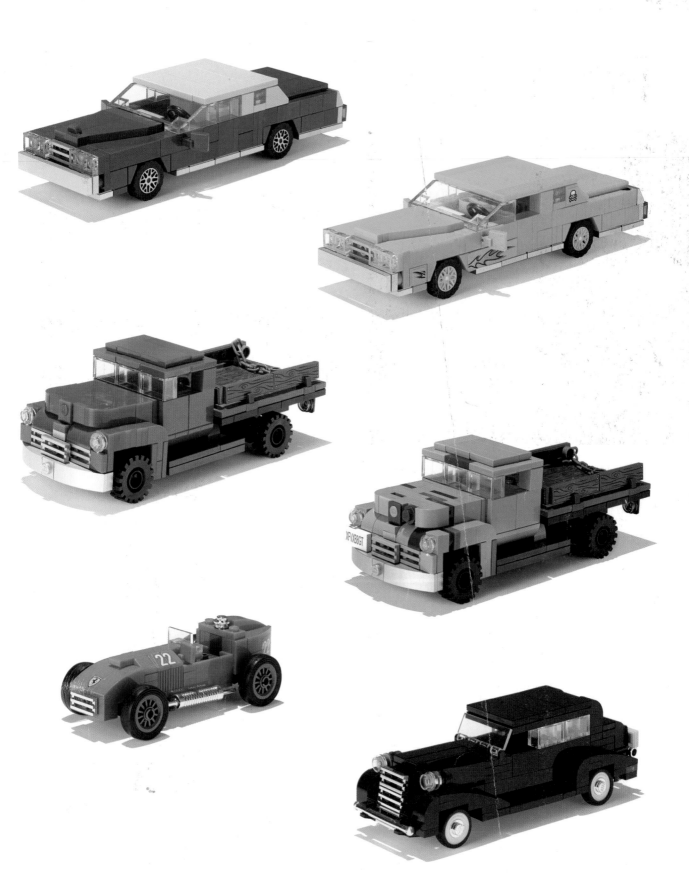

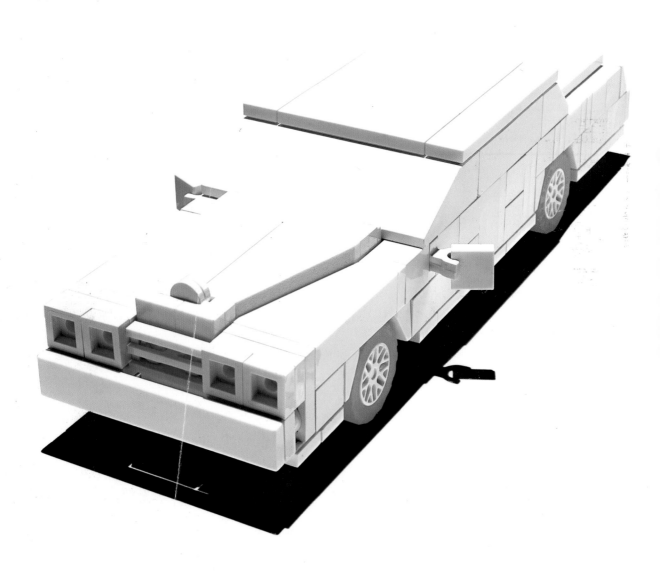